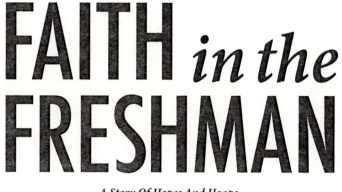

FAITH *in the* FRESHMAN

A Story Of Hopes And Hoops

FAITH *in the* FRESHMAN

A Story Of Hopes And Hoops

Patrick Ferry

Book Design by James Saleska

Pat Keenan, President
W1332 Elmwood Avenue
Ixonia, WI 53036

ISBN: 978-0-9821120-0-7

To Tammy—when our kids grow up, I hope they turn out just like you!

ACKNOWLEDGEMENTS

It is such fun to be part of a terrific team. In the past I have been stuck on some really bad teams. No doubt I contributed my share to whatever caused us to perform so poorly. An advantage, I suppose, of having been a part of teams that were so unbelievably lousy is a keener sense of appreciation for the chance to be part of one that is exceptionally good. The team that has assisted me with this project has been remarkable. Most of us have had no previous experience with writing a book—ours has been a "freshman" story in more ways than one. I take responsibility for whatever rookie mistakes have been made. The rest of the team, however, deserves full credit for volunteering the time and energy, as well as inspiring the ideas and insights, that now bring us as far as we have come.

Two people in particular got me thinking about actually taking the time to try and translate the frequently told oral version of one of my stories into written form. Perhaps Allen Prochnow and Diane

Kulkarni would have been less encouraging had they known that they would in turn be asked to read the unpolished initial draft of the manuscript. Their support for the writing never waned, and I am grateful for their enthusiasm. Similarly, Tom Saleska's patience and persistence in plowing through material that was far from a finished form is also much appreciated. Since he is so closely related to me and my subject matter on several levels, nobody was better positioned to help me sort everything out from the beginning than Tom. He took to the task without prodding and without plodding.

The second wave of readers included Jim Juergensen and Rick Riehl. Each has poured over more than his fair share of student essays through their many years of experience as master teachers. Their proofreading was invaluable. Much more meaningful, however, were our engaging conversations about the fine art of parenting stimulated by their reading and my writing. My great respect and admiration for both of them made me covet their reaction and advice. What they generously offered made the entire experience worthwhile for me.

Books are their business, but a book like this represents a bit of a new venture for Pat and Alison Keenan and Green Tree Publishers. From the outset they have happily embraced the effort and have been incredibly affirmative. They believe in this book and have been willing to make its publication possible. The extent to which this book finds its way to readers outside of my limited orbit of family and friends is due in large part to Anita Clark and Chris Johnson. Each of them continues generously to lend marketing expertise and communications skills to the endeavor.

My assistant, Lynne Schroeder, has the rather challenging daily job of trying to keep me in line and on task. Along with her normal duties,

Lynne has assisted with this project on her own time. She has played an indispensable role in nearly every facet of the work.

No one has worked more earnestly or thought more creatively about the final production of this book than James Saleska. James probably had no idea what he was getting himself into when he first expressed interest in being involved in layout and design. I have a hunch we are barely scratching the surface of his extraordinary gifts and talents.

Without Andrew Ferry I would have only every other chapter of this book. Indeed, without Andrew the story is incomplete. Along with providing some excellent material for so many pages, Andrew was himself the most eager reader of the first draft of every section. I will always be his biggest fan. It has been a great experience to have him rooting for me from one chapter to the next.

Without Tammy Ferry there would be no book at all. She read and re-read most iterations of the manuscript. She balanced constructive criticism and positive feedback. She listened patiently as I droned on and on about ideas I was considering. But, more than anything else, Tammy has lived much of the story with me. She has been the inspiration for most of what has been good. She has been a steady balance when things have fared less well. Tammy has been God's wonderful gift in our lives, and our five children and I are grateful to God for her. Proverbs 31:28 comes to mind when we think of Tammy: "Her children rise up and call her blessed; her husband also, and he praises her."

Finally, I acknowledge with words inadequate to express my appreciation my father, Lefty, and my sainted mother, Billie Ferry. The older I get, the more I realize what genuinely fine and truly loving people raised me. I can only hope that a little of who they were rubbed off on me as a parent of Peter, Hannah, Andrew, Rachel, and Stephen.

PREFACE

Most rites of passage, by definition, are experiences we go through but once, and there is normally no turning back. Some of our regular routines may qualify as rituals, but uncommon are the rites marking critical turning points that vividly distinguish the end of one chapter of our lives and the start of the next.

Within my own professional routine I participate in an especially poignant rite of passage, and I do it over and over again. For each year of the past two decades, as late summer begins to turn to early autumn, I have witnessed a moment that never fails to touch the lives of eighteen-year-olds about to take a very big step. Of course, many years ago, when I was their age, I went through it myself. Nowadays my function is to help usher them forward. They are kids leaving home and heading off to college.

It is part of my job as a university president to be present at freshman orientation to welcome young women and men and their mothers and fathers to campus. Every kid sitting in the audience before me has a story. The adult sitting on either side of each son or daughter is usually familiar with many of the details. To a greater or lesser degree parents helped develop the plot up to this point. From here, though, moms and dads sense that not only their day-to-day oversight but also their broader parental influence diminishes. Our children have been raised for precisely this moment. When the time arrives, however, it is seldom easy to let go.

None of them, neither parents nor their children, knows all that lies ahead. There is, nevertheless, the sense that the once far-off future has nearly arrived. This rite of passage is at once exhilarating and terrifying, joyful and painful. It would be easy enough to approach the task of addressing them as just one other duty to perform and then simply move on to whatever is next on my agenda. Few things that I do, however, seem as significant to me as the ten or fifteen minutes I have to speak to new students their first day on campus. I am eager for their stories to have happy endings, though I know it is not always possible. At the very least, I am determined to have their college experience get off to a good start. My goal is to do whatever I can to assure students and their parents that the journey before them, wherever it leads, is almost always worth that next step.

It might be helpful for incoming freshmen to discover that I was a freshman once too—albeit long, long ago in a place far, far away. Maybe I can relate to them, at least a little. I am not a freshman any longer, but I am a father. I processed what being a freshman meant for me a while back, but being a father is still very much a work in progress. Since it is much fresher than the freshman stuff, I am not always so sure about what I am doing and feel a bit vulnerable. I know other parents feel the same way. I always try to leave the impression that when it comes to the rite of passage of sending kids off to college, I am the professional and can be trusted to provide reliable counsel. Pushing others toward the unfolding future, I have found, is lots easier than striding confidently toward it myself.

As my own children began to reach eighteen, I appreciated more fully how parents feel about the impact of this rite of passage. While I have always found the occasion sentimental and even deeply moving, suddenly it all struck close to home—very close. Now my sons and daughters were the ones heading off to college, and the impact on me was jolting. Indeed, from the day the first college recruitment letter arrived in our mailbox the entire process took on new meaning. My parents faced this situation three decades ago, but at the time I was too preoccupied with adapting to my changing reality to worry or even wonder how they were dealing with the way these changes affected them. Revisiting their reactions and my own recollections of those days interests me more as I try to come to terms with the unfolding of my children's stories today.

One way of relating to freshman and their parents, as well as to the children related to me because I am their parent, is my story. Some of what follows is the expanded version of my freshman orientation oration. Indeed, the recounting of my own freshman year experience is often the centerpiece of public presentations I make before all sorts of audiences as often as I have opportunity. It is my stump speech, and I regularly tell it in one form or another at most stops where my itinerary takes me. The applicability is surprisingly transferable, and I have learned ways to connect the message to all kinds of occasions. Since most of my presentations have something to do with higher education and its impact on the lives of young people, not much twisting or contorting is necessary to bridge from my story to the appointed theme.

My story did not go according to my plan. With the benefit of hindsight, I am grateful for the change of direction. That was by no means the way that I felt when I first left home, and the path ahead was anything but clear to me at the time. Part of being a freshman is figuring things out, I suppose. It took me a while. In some ways I am still interpreting that year's significance. But, the only way possible for me to describe who I am today (for better or for worse) or why I do what I do (for good or for ill) is to refer to my freshman year in college. Hearers have often told me how much they enjoy listening to the story. I am finally following up on the frequent suggestion to put it all on paper.

The other part of my story has been requested by no one. This is the more clandestine and covert material of my private persona. Until now I have kept it mostly to myself. I am reluctant to divulge too much about my private life, although glimpses no doubt have slipped out from time to time. A college presidency includes responsibilities that are often very public in nature. To have as much visibility as possible on campus and in the broader community goes with the job. Fair enough. But, before I am a college president I am a husband and father, and much less of what I do in those roles is so well known. Being too transparent as a parent may not benefit my image, and I have a reputation to uphold! Still, in this book, and in my life, I am a father first. That will not be a big secret—in these pages I am apparent.

I am also a historian. Understanding the past has always been more comfortable territory for me than exploring the untamed future. Yet, I realize that autobiographical material is not necessarily the most reliable record of the past, and a memoir such as this is part of a genre in which blurring lines between history and good story is accepted. My attempt to avoid too much bias and to tell my story without all of the embellishment that memory invariably (and inaccurately) recreates has been to make considerable use of source materials readily at my disposal. Letters, newspaper articles, photographs, and journal entries preserved in inordinately good order for more than thirty years have finally been put to some constructive use! That being said, my goal has been more to tell a good story than to write a good history. A memoir draws much from memory, and I use documents and other evidence to supplement recall more than the reverse.

This story is about basketball, but only incidentally. That does not mean basketball is inconsequential. Indeed, without basketball I might still have a few stories to tell, but I am not sure which ones they would be. This much is clear: without basketball none of them could possibly be my story. I love to read other stories about basketball, particularly ones that tell tales of unsung heroes from unfamiliar settings. Lots of great basketball stories have been the inspiration for many fine books. Basketball-related material fills most of the pages that follow in this book, too. But, basketball is not the point, not really. It is a magical game that has provided a backdrop for my dreams. I have found it to be a sport that too often brings me face to face with reality. For every winner there is a loser. For every victor there is the vanquished. Losing, I believe, always teaches us more than winning. I have been taught a lot. Most significantly, through basketball I have learned what Saint Paul meant when he says that we are "more than conquerors."

This story, therefore, is about faith, though not always explicitly. Faith, however, is intrinsic throughout. Faith awakened, faith formed, faith challenged, faith questioned, faith ignored, faith affirmed—without faith I might have other stories to relate about myself, but I'm not so certain. This much is sure: without faith the stories I may tell would not be mine. I am encouraged whenever I hear others share their own stories of faith, especially ordinary people living out everyday lives. Of course, great stories of faith have inspired many books. This one is not the story of a saint marching from victory unto victory until every foe is vanquished. How I'd love to be in that number! Instead, I continue to find that the passage from darkness to light does not remove gray areas from the path before me. Often I stumble. There is no turning back, however, and I am anxious—with equal parts anxiety and excitement—to see what comes next. I'm taking the next step of the journey, wherever it leads, in faith.

"MIDNIGHT SPECIAL"
CHAPTER 1

August 1977—A midnight snack and the *Midnight Special.* Nothing was special about the snack. Whatever the refrigerator rendered would suffice so long as it was an ample portion. An eighteen-year-old body craves the kind of abundance that a man with a middle-aged metabolism unwisely dares to sustain. Cold pizza, hot dogs, sandwich stuff, anything that was readily available and easily accessible. Cookies, chocolate cake, even fresh fruit if pickings were slim. Some dessert was obviously required. To call it only a snack was an inadequate understatement of what typically was the day's fourth meal. Typical, however, is by definition not special.

The *Midnight Special,* by contrast, was much more than a mere staple for another appetite—a teenager's taste for music. Record shops sold us our record albums, but in days before music video the chance not only to hear but also see an artist or band was a treat. Seeing and hearing a pop song sung live was a special treat. Friday nights in the

'70s, once Johnnie Carson signed off and much of America went to bed, the *Midnight Special* aired live musical acts on NBC. No longer interested enough to rise early for Saturday morning's cartoons, teens like me stayed up an hour-and-a-half past midnight (with every intention of sleeping in until noon) and got glimpses of our guitar heroes. Nearly everybody who was anybody in the '70s made an appearance on the program.

ABBA, AC/DC, Aerosmith ... the list was long ... B.B. King, Beach Boys, Bee Gees ... live TV was a good stage ... Village People, War, Warren Zevon—the *Midnight Special* had us covered from A to ZZ Top. A relaxed curfew after high school graduation in the summer of 1977 made catching Wolfman Jack's howling intro less of a priority. Rare, however, was the Friday night that ran late enough to make me miss the entire ninety-minute episode.

That same extended curfew allegedly hindered my parents' ability to relax. Sleep was fitful, they claimed, until they knew that I was home in one piece. The rafter-raising, hardly harmonious snoring duet from the bedroom upstairs belied that claim. If the volume was raised high enough on the TV to stir either of them from the cacophonous slumber, and if my parents could hear Johnnie Rivers crooning about the "Midnight Special shining its ever-loving light on me," then maybe the two of them could rest a little easier knowing that their son was no longer out on the town. With a plate full of complimentary kitchen concessions before me and my front row seat on the couch reserved even if I arrived late for the show, I sat down to listen, and to watch, and to eat. Billie and Lefty could roll over and resume their rest.

Billie and Lefty—once a Jefferson High School teacher commented that such names gave the impression that our family was being run by a couple of gangsters. Anything else that I learned in Mr. Jensen's English class has since been forgotten. But, his passing comment that my mom and dad might have something in common with Bonnie and Clyde has long lingered. Mr. Jensen was right, of course. Billie and Lefty do make good names for gangsters. No one who knew them, least of all me, could have imagined any association between my folks and organized or even disorganized crime. Their vices were few. Neither drank, at least not much, and their shared addiction to nicotine hardly separated them from many adults of their generation. For entertainment they played pinochle once a month with other couples who had been good friends for decades. No high stakes in these card games.

Now and then they took the rest of us out to dinner. We'd dine at the Howard Johnson's, where my father ordered clams, more, I think, because they reminded him of growing up in New England than because he had a hankering for seafood. Lefty ended up in Colorado and became a bricklayer after the war. By plying his trade he brought home enough to pay the bills and keep the refrigerator adequately stocked to feed his family—even four meals a day on some Fridays. Billie stayed home to manage things and care for her four children, who were born in shifts. The two older boys were twelve and eight years older than me. My little sister was two years younger. We never did without, but there was never much extra. Any discretionary dollars Dad earned were squirreled away for trips to New Hampshire to visit his side of the family. Four times we traveled "back east" before I graduated from high school. Once we made the whole trip by train. Otherwise, we never left the state and seldom even ventured beyond our side of town. Theirs could have been a perfect cover for going gangster except their names might have given them away. Law-abiding Billie and Lefty mostly minded their own business and stuck close to home.

That made this Friday night especially atypical. In the morning Billie, Lefty, and I were taking another road trip. There would be no sleeping in until noon. Any sleep at all, as it turned out, would have been more than I actually got. *Midnight Special* only managed to keep my attention for a little while. I watched the bands but lacked focus. I could hear the tunes but didn't really listen. I devoured some leftovers but more out of habit than hunger. The TV went off before the final act. Once my dish was down to crumbs I called it a night and went upstairs to bed. No surprise, my parents were sound asleep and the sounds of their sleep reverberated from their room into the hallway. I listened to them snore, sometimes in unison, more often independent of one another, but between them nearly unabated until darkness was chased away by daylight. They rested, but I was restive. On this night sleep was fitful for me. Snoring from across the hall, however, was not to blame for keeping me awake.

Lack of preparation was not the problem either. The Granada was in the driveway gassed up and loaded down. All the essentials were packed. The prized album collection, which numbered over a hundred long-playing records, was safely cushioned in the trunk along with the already antiquated but only recently inherited stereo equipment. The entire system was handed down to me from my brother after his upgrade. My records deserved better, but higher quality sound was beyond my means.

I did not scrimp, however, on the Raleigh racing bike with its rock-hard saddle and skinny tires. I spent over $100 of hard-earned and frugally saved money from my summer job. The bicycle was tied tight and secured atop the car. This would be my transportation once the Granada was unloaded and made its return trip to the driveway. Unless I chose to walk somewhere, so just in case I also packed shoes. Somewhere in the suitcase were the four pairs of Chuck Taylor Converse All-Stars. The canvas high-tops that I wore until they were beyond worn out included one pair each of traditional white and traditional black—the colors worn since the shoe was introduced; Jefferson High red—the school color, along with gray of what so recently had become my *alma mater;* and emerald green—suitable for a kid with a name as Irish as mine. The rainbow of optional shades was introduced by Converse in the late '70s. Soon enough a pair of orange ones would be added to my closet.

The brand new bedspread, meanwhile, was colored somewhere between calico and camouflage. Billie and Bev Lessing bought mine to match the one that Bev's son and my friend, Reed, would be using. In another day it would cover my bunk, but in the driveway the bedspread, along with sheets, towels and anything else that could be stuffed, were shoved into corners to make it all fit. The back seat strategically was left empty, allowing space for my body to sprawl out and compensate for the deprivation suffered through the previous long night.

The Granada was all set; that was not the problem. Sleep was lacking—not because we weren't set to travel, but because I was not ready. The preference to stick close to home must have been genetic. I didn't want to go. I was not ready, and I knew it already.

Kansas? Our ten-hour trek did not rival the longer expeditions to visit Dad's relatives, only a single long day's drive in the car, but that left enough time to ask the question—repeatedly. Kansas? It was a fair enough question and deserved to be asked over and again, though silently, of course, in order not to evoke any discussion on the subject. Billie realized that she risked probing too deeply to wonder out loud. Better to stick fairly close to the surface and settle for superficial than to get under somebody's acne-challenged skin. Find other things about which to chat or even quibble, she understood, rather than stumble into awkward places where mothers and their eighteen-year-old sons simply do not want to go together. Sensitive places like, "Can I bear to let you go?" Uncomfortable places like, "Are you sure this is the right thing to do?" Places like Kansas.

Leaving the Kansas question off her lips and confining it under her breath at least offered slight distraction from scenery that was hardly scenic. The windows were rolled down—air conditioning was an unnecessary extravagance when Lefty was in the market for a used car. This worked well enough in Denver's mild and dry summer climate, but it was hotter and more humid in Kansas. Opened windows stirred a breeze, not a cool one, but air at least moved.

Nothing, however, could be done to improve the view of wheat fields bordering more wheat fields in unbroken succession for mile after monotonous mile. Sights competed with sound in what seemed a conspiracy to make the trip more unpleasant. Getting air to move inside the car meant acquiescing to mind-numbing noise. Wind sucked in the unrelenting roar and rattle that was the price to pay for relief from suffocating and stagnant air. Even if a decent FM radio station could be found, a long shot given our place on the map, listening was futile. Neither chatting nor quibbling proved worth the effort. She could not hear herself think, but Billie thought anyway. She kept her thoughts, and her questions, to herself. What else could she do? Little to see and hard to hear—finding ways to pass the time were severely limited.

I found one way. The maddening straight line that stretched I-70 from Denver's airport and halfway across the tediously plain Great Plains transformed the frustration of missed sleep the night before into the next day's opportunity. We settled into our roles. Dad drove across, Mom mulled over, and I slept through Kansas.

To the extent that the place was mentioned at all, Coloradans arrogantly referred to Kansas only in jest. To most people where I am from, put more directly, Kansas was a joke. I always regarded Nebraska contemptuously but spoke of Kansas only dismissively. Passing through for some travelers was an unhappy but inescapable portion of an itinerary that hopefully led somewhere more appealing. Going on purpose, by contrast, and with the idea of staying beyond a few day's visit to unfortunate relatives who inexplicably inextricably lived in Kansas defied understanding. Billie was a second-generation Denver native, and I was a third. Our predisposition to look down our nose on Kansas from a mile high was as much inherited as our preference to stay put in Colorado. Dorothy's famous insight, "there is no place like home," drew no argument from either of us, but we gleefully gloated that her home was not ours. Any little misgivings that Billie might have harbored before we disembarked from our driveway swelled into much larger apprehensions early into the trip.

Lefty focused on the task at hand. Had they actually been gangsters, their duties would have been clearly defined. Billie was the brains. Lefty was the driver. She was a thinker, and he was a doer. He was a man who worked with his hands all day long, and they bore the calluses of many years of lifting rough-edged brick and stone. Lefty's own occasionally exhibited rough edge fooled no one. My father was marshmallow—soft on the inside and always willing to offer a beat-up hand to help anybody. He knew no stranger, and Lefty's personality oozed a sort of childlike sweetness and simplicity that easily endeared him to others. People who met him for the first time quickly figured out that he was at once extraordinarily kind and eccentrically one-of-a-kind, very soft-hearted and a little wrong-headed.

Being the driver never deterred Lefty from steering himself straight into the center of discussions and debates where even angels feared to tread. He rushed to voice his peculiar angle on virtually any subject and with greater relish if his opinion both rubbed wrong and also threw a spotlight his direction. His grandstanding sometimes drove Billie to distraction. In fact, my mother refused to sit with Lefty in the grandstands at the high school when they watched their children compete for the Jefferson Saints in the games that our father taught us to play. I guess sometimes he embarrassed her, and when he did, Billie never felt the slightest reservation about whether to hold her own tongue when it came to her husband's unrefined remarks or lack of sophistication.

Eugene was his given name. It meant *well-born,* but it was less apt a descriptor than his nickname. Not adroit, Lefty was never bothered by being sort of a *gauche* guy. It fit him like his well-worn left-handed baseball glove. Billie did not pretend to be well born either, but the best way to be protected from guilt by association was to be the first to draw attention to his sometimes silliness. Usually he just let it pass. Constant correction, however, eventually became an irritant to him. Argument, as a result, became too common a form of conversation between them. Unwitting attempts to out-snore each other as they slept were followed by a more willful and well-rehearsed pattern of trying to outwit one another during waking hours. It was never really much of a contest. Lefty was smart enough to know that Billie was unlikely to give in, so he normally backed down first. Billie felt it was her responsibility to keep Lefty in check.

Billie kept Lefty in Colorado, too. They met dancing in Denver near the end of World War II at the military base where he was stationed once his tour of Europe, courtesy of the United States Air Force, was completed. Soon after they met they married. He never imagined that it would be only the first such trip when Lefty took his bride back to New Hampshire with plans to remain there permanently. They didn't stay long. Maybe she snapped her fingers. Possibly she raised her voice. Perhaps she clicked her heels. However she managed to make her point, the message was clear—there is no place like home, and she did not mean Kansas. Lefty deferred to Billie, and they headed back to Denver to make Colorado home. He took the wheel, and she gave directions. Lefty was the driver and Billie was the mastermind.

Those roles did not change. But, if he had any opinion about Kansas, as my father drove the Granada across the state, he uncharacteristically kept it quiet. Maybe there was too much noise to bother starting an argument or even a conversation. Or, possibly their silence on the subject hinted at an uncommon concurrence. Who could argue? It was plain as the Plains could be. Kansas was a joke, but not a very humorous one.

Lefty faced one other unfortunate reality that made adding commentary to the hot air already overwhelming the inside of the car needless. My father could not relate to what I was thinking, even though he was so closely related to me. Surely some of this was the usual chasm that men and boys of different generations find difficult to bridge. Lefty liked to come close to quoting Mark Twain by saying the older I got, the smarter he got. Supposedly this would become clearer to me as over time I more fully realized the breadth of his wisdom and appreciated the depth of his insight. Frankly, as might most teenagers, I doubted this day would ever come. Occasionally he made me wince. Like many kids my age I worried that an out-of-touch parent could prove damaging to me in my social circle. I need not have fretted. My friends liked Lefty a lot, and the same antics that caused Billie to cringe and me to cower only made them giggle. Mom and I made the mistake of taking Lefty seriously in a way that nobody else did and of allowing that driver sometimes to drive us both crazy.

Unlike Billie, I seldom took time to talk, much less to argue, with him. Of course, should a need for a skirmish ever suddenly arise he gladly took opposing positions simply because they were not mine. But, Lefty didn't really want to fight with me either. Billie gave him sufficient trouble to keep his sparring skills honed, and he'd had more than enough father-son scuffling from all the years that he'd gone nose-to-nose with his own dad. Lefty vowed to be different from his father, and for good reason. Eugene Sr. was no more well born than his son.

What little money he earned was squandered, and Grandpa Ferry made it his practice to move his family to new digs about as often as the rent was due. Luckily Lefty's resemblances to my grandfather were unrecognizable. Unlike Eugene the Elder, Eugene the Younger worked hard, stayed sober, and supported his wife and children. Despite coming home dog-tired after laying brick from just after sunrise until near sundown he bounded the stairs to wash up, hurried to the table to chow down, and then spent a couple hours most evenings over at the field, or on the diamond, or in the gym coaching practice sessions for nearly every little league team on which his kids ever played. When players from those same teams later took the field or the hardwood at Jefferson High School, Lefty proudly claimed some fair share of the credit.

Difficult to imagine that the man who took such pride teaching countless Colorado kids how to throw a tight spiral, or how to slide into second, or how to shoot a lay-up could become somewhat distant from his own son even before the boy went away to Kansas. The chance to become well acquainted with the one player on his team who lived under his own roof, even by way of an occasional heated discussion, was like air conditioning in a used car—it didn't get hot enough to bother. He loved me. I never once doubted that he did. I loved him, too, but the older I got, the less I figured that he knew about me. We didn't argue, but we rarely had an in-depth discussion either. Meeting halfway should have been easy enough for us both, but now I was heading in a completely different direction, and my father was driving me there.

If he had something to say about Kansas, I wasn't listening. With the wind roaring and rattling I couldn't have heard him anyway. Besides, I was sleeping, and I stayed asleep right up until the exit ramp at Salina, smack dab in the middle of Kansas, approached at last. Lefty mindlessly prepared to execute the turn to adjust our route and point us southward toward our destination. Despite so many consecutive miles of straight ahead, the driver had not forgotten how to maneuver his vehicle and steer the Granada—Lefty turned right. The self-appointed navigator seated beside him made absolutely sure that the man behind the wheel was well informed about the pending southerly shift. She had been looking forward to the change of direction, if not a change of scenery, for hours. He dutifully activated the blinker, which, along with

Billie's carefully voiced instructions, could now be faintly heard from the backseat once the car began to slow and the noisy breeze slightly diminished. The little bit of commotion was enough to interrupt the nap of their passenger. In his rearview mirror Lefty may have noticed me stir, but he was not privy to what stirred within me. He could see that I had been sleeping, but my father was not allowed access to my dreams. I never opened a window wide enough for him to have a good look inside of me.

Were it not for Lefty, however, the contours of those dreams probably would have followed along other lines. He gave my dreams their original shape. In a household where a father loves sports as much as my dad did, the children might reasonably be expected to play along—particularly when no other interests are being cultivated. I never carried hod to help him build a fireplace or finish a patio job that he occasionally did on the side to earn a little extra vacation cash. When he got under the hood of the Granada to have a look, or underneath to change the oil, I conveniently found something else to do. No nudge was necessary, however, to get me, my brothers before me, or my sister after me into the fun of games. Playing in big games someday, for Jefferson High School and beyond, became the recurring theme of my dreams, or at least of my delusions.

For Billie sport was an acquired taste. She was no athlete, but she became a connoisseur of athletics who, like her husband, arranged most of her weekly calendar around her sons' or daughter's practice schedules. Meals needed to be ready on time and early enough to be digested before competition began. Equipment appropriate for the given season had to be situated where it could predictably be gathered without resort to a last-minute frantic search. Uniforms had to be washed and looking sharp because appearing disheveled or slovenly on game day was not acceptable. Cleats might be polished up and used for a couple of years for baseball or football. But, before a basketball was ever rolled out on to the floor to launch the year's first practice some spanking new Chuck Taylor All-Stars had to be purchased. These tasks and so many others fell to her. Billie was an indispensable role player who always came through. Competitors and coaches who execute as reliably and efficiently as she performed are surely destined for the Hall of Fame. Glory, though, was never her goal. Billie devotedly played her part on the sidelines so that when the games began she could sit in the bleachers with the other moms and just watch.

Billie watched her children compete and rooted for them to do well, and she watched her husband coach and hoped that he would not make too much a spectacle of himself. She was a fan. She was our fan. She was my fan. As a fan who was also a mom, Billie did not confine herself to cheering us on as we played. Billie also understood me.

We did not always agree. Though a distant runner-up, I was without a doubt her second most familiar familial antagonist. For all of our squabbling, however, Billie left no question about her keen interest in whatever I was doing, in whatever was on my mind, in me. Thanks to Lefty I was not even close to being her favorite target to engage in argument. Nor, for that matter, was "favorite" a word that she likely would ever have applied to me if coaxed or coerced to tell the truth. By my considered calculation I placed about fourth-most favorite out of four among her children. Bob was so handsome. Bill was so funny. Kim was her baby and only daughter. Meanwhile, she referred to me as her "nemesis." But, fourth out of four was better than nothing, and Billie had more than enough to go around for all of us.

Billie was not only related to me, she was connected to me. She knew my dream and never tried to stop me from trying to make it come true. Without Lefty the dream would never have been mine. Without Billie I would never have had the courage to try. Thankfully, she held her breath and didn't ask me, "Was I sure this is right thing to do?" Kansas was the one place that offered me a chance to find out. Ready or not, and I felt no readier on the southbound ramp at Salina than I did in our Denver driveway, I was on my way to discover for myself whether this really was the right turn.

Late Saturday afternoon Lefty aimed the Granada toward the bridge that crossed over the Walnut River into Winfield. Billie's mood began to lighten almost immediately. No doubt there was relief at having finally reached our much anticipated destination, but there was more. Winfield, it turns out, had a charm that she would never have suspected based on observations of other small Kansas towns along the highway. To be fair, the perspective from the interstate shows only the edges of the cities it slips past, often the seedier outskirts, and offers a view that does no place justice. Still, Winfield's exceptionally warm welcome was not due to the unbearably hot, muggy August afternoon. Indeed, in spite of the weather, all of her thoughts about Kansas suddenly seemed subject to review. Put simply, she liked the look.

Lefty blurted out that it reminded him of New England. "Everything reminded him of New England," I sarcastically whispered to myself, but rather than clobber him with a rebuke, Billie, to my surprise, agreed with him. Had I thought about it longer, I might have better under-stood their reaction. Lefty grew up moving from one New Hampshire town to the next, while Billie's much shorter stint after their wedding, when she was about my age, was the first and last time in her life that she lived anywhere other than Denver. The only experience either of them ever had with small towns was in New England.

There are features, to be sure, that many small towns have in common, and whichever ones this Kansas town shared with Thornton Wilder's fictional *Our Town* or other real-life New Hampshire villages evoked their first-glance assessment. Maybe it was the prominence of City Hall near the confluence of the two main drags, Main Street and Ninth Avenue, with competing banks on opposite corners. The banks anchored a scattering of shops, stores, bars, and restaurants up and down the block. Maybe it was the stately old homes with their sprawling wraparound front porches standing side-by-side for the better part of a mile along Ninth Avenue. Or, maybe it was the trees. The previous several hours of our expedition had been devoid not only of trees but also of the much vaunted sunflowers that were conspicuous by their absence along our route. Winfield, by contrast, deserved its self-proclaimed designation as the "City of Trees." A canopy of elms lined Ninth Avenue and created a shadowy passageway for our processional and an all-too-brief escape from the oppressive heat.

There was something about the quaint scene that conjured images in each of their minds that reminded them of the spot where they traveled to start their lives together three decades earlier. Now I was starting out on my own. Whether Winfield resembled New England did not make a whit of difference to me, so I just took their word for it. Their apparent attraction to the place and whatever happy reminders it may have brought to them did little to calm my discomfort. After all, their experiment living in New Hampshire didn't last very long. Besides, I was the one who would be left behind in Winfield, Kansas. Warm welcome or not, before anybody got too cozy with the idea of me sticking around in this hot, sticky town, I was already scheming about how best to shorten my stay and go home. She could keep her Kansas, but Dorothy surely had it right, there is no place like home.

This time Lefty turned left from Ninth Avenue onto College Street and my eyes were opened wide as the place that definitely was not home but where I would be left behind came into view. The road got its name for good reason. In fact, there were two colleges on College Street within walking distance of each other. Southwestern College, the bigger of the two schools with an enrollment of six hundred or so students, was more than twice the size of tiny St. John's College down the street. St. John's was our target, and remaining wide-eyed was crucial since a blink might mean missing the place altogether.

If Winfield was charming and quaint, St. John's only added to the impression for my mother. Big-city Billie was being transformed into a Chamber of Commerce spokesperson for small towns and small colleges from out of nowhere. Indeed, "nowhere" struck me as the right term. Geographically, Salina may have been the middle of Kansas, but I was now more convinced than ever Winfield was the middle of nowhere. Billie's optimism continued to surge even as my doubts redoubled. The school's mascot was the Eagle, but I wasn't exactly soaring. She sensed my flagging spirit and sought to prop me up. The students were called Johnnies, and like it or not, I was about to become a Johnnie myself. To give it the old college try meant I would at least have to try St. John's College. We both knew that I had no other choice.

The few buildings that dotted the campus looked collegiate enough, and the grounds included some of the trees that contributed to Winfield's renown. Billie sat in the shade of one of them and downed a can of pop, which she drank as infrequently as alcohol, just to cool herself down after lugging some boxes upstairs. She fanned her face in futility while Lefty and I continued to unpack the Granada and place my belongings in the same room where my pal Reed had already established squatter's rights. The Lessings arrived in Winfield ahead of us, and Bev made up Reed's bed with the spread that was twin to the one shoved in the Granada's trunk and among the last things carried from the car into the room.

Back home the Lessings lived around the block, and Reed and I had been friends since junior high school. My initial pathway to St. John's was fairly circuitous, which meant Reed's route was downright obscure. His familiarity with this small college started with me. Once my plans began to solidify I started encouraging Reed to consider coming along to Winfield. For me, having a roommate from my own neighborhood would surely alleviate some of my apprehensions about being dropped off in Kansas. I would have somebody who missed the mountains, who rooted for the Broncos, and who loved Colorado as much as I did. Reed, at least, could commiserate. Given that he had no other definitive arrangements, and I guess nothing better to do, he talked it over with his parents and then, almost unbelievably, he signed up.

I knew all of the reasons that I was eager for Reed to be my roommate. It was harder to understand why he might wish to stay in the same quarters with me. Boys often have strange ways of showing their affection and appreciation for one another during adolescence and into early adulthood. Sometimes it is insecurity, usually it is immaturity, but young men have a proclivity to be rough on each other. Once in awhile that manifests itself in roughhousing—the wrestling and jostling that are at once tests of strength and also release of hormonal tension. Perhaps more painful are the verbal jousts through which one-upmanship comes in the form of teasing and tormenting. Reed was my friend, and I enjoyed being around him. But, I was merciless in my treatment of him. In middle school he was sort of the runt of our crowd, and I derived too much pleasure at his expense. My quick wit and sharp tongue was something most of the others found humorous, and I played to the audience even if it meant Reed was continually skewered by my barbs. By high school the ribbing relented a lot, but not completely. Frankly, I am not sure why Reed even liked me, much less why he would come with me to Kansas and live in the same dormitory space. When I got to Rehwinkel Hall, Reed was already there and waiting for me. Overjoyed to see him, I wrestled him to the ground.

There was barely enough time to get stuff settled in and sweat showered off before freshmen and their families convened in the Centennial Campus Center for a welcome banquet. No assigned seats, we considered saving a place for the Lessings and hoped that by dining next to them we might avoid a little of the awkwardness of dinner with complete strangers. Nearly everybody in the room fit into that same category, but others gave the impression of being much more at ease. Billie, Lefty, and I did not have much experience with banquets. When out to dinner back home at the Howard Johnson's, small talk with others nearby was unnecessary and unexpected. Lefty ate his clams, put a tip on the table for the waitress, and paid the cashier, and we went home. Simply minding your own business at this event, however, lacked social grace and was unthinkable. So why not make it easy and chat with folks that you already knew? The Lessings, however, were late.

More precisely, we were early. We were always early. Whenever we went anywhere Billie and Lefty got dressed and ready and then spent fifteen minutes stirring anxiously in the living room with an eye fixed on the clock until deciding that they might as well go. For all their fretting about not wishing to be late Billie and Lefty always arrived long before anybody else no matter the destination. Now I feared we would undoubtedly pay for our promptness.

Sure enough, as we waited for the Lessings another family scooted into chairs to sit down across the table from us. We took a breath, braced ourselves, and made our best attempt at etiquette, which was never Lefty's forte. Her name was Laura, and she was with her parents John and Helen Rolf. She looked more like her mother than her father, I thought, probably because he was bald. The small talk was interrupted almost before it began by an invitation to prayer. Compared to prebanquet banter, prayer was even more unfamiliar and uncommon territory for me and my parents, so praying in Kansas made me feel doubly out of place. I peeked for just long enough to see that the Rolfs knew what they were doing. Next I noticed the prefix "Rev." in front of John Rolf's name. Laura was a preacher's kid.

Like me, she was also an eighteen-year-old freshman. Also like me, Laura was shy, and we did not say a word to each other the entire time. Casual conversation was left up to our parents. If we'd had access to each other's birth certificates Laura and I would have found that we were born the very same day. There was no need to examine one another's driver's licenses for our families to discover that we also shared the same hometown and lived within a couple miles of each other near Denver. Such a small world, and right there in such a small town. The Rolfs had made the same long trip across I-70 to Salina, south through Wichita and on into Winfield. The next morning John and Helen and

Lefty and Billie would retrace their route and head back home—without Laura, and, much worse, without me. The thought of it stung.

When the banquet mercifully ended Billie and Lefty got into the Granada and only backtracked as far as Main Street. They checked into the Camelot Inn, where they would undoubtedly sleep soundly, snoring resoundingly all night long after their very long day. They could relax knowing their son was situated and where he was supposed to be. But, I was far from convinced that Winfield, Kansas, and St. John's College was where I belonged.

While other incoming freshmen were corralled to mingle in "icebreaker" activities arranged for them by very outgoing sophomores, I escaped from the group, unchained my Raleigh from the rack outside the dormitory, and rode that racing bike as fast as I could peddle. Like a laser, I went straight to the Camelot Inn. The Granada, scads of Kansan bugs plastered all over the front grille and windshield but otherwise emptied, was parked in the lot. Billie and Lefty were in their room with the window-unit air conditioner turned on high. I wanted to knock on their door. I wanted to go inside. I wanted to go home. I wasn't ready, and I knew that already. What was I doing here? I had been bewitched by a dream, bedeviled by a delusion. Now I just wanted to wake up at home in my own bed, in my own house, and not in Kansas anymore.

Tears dribbled down my cheeks as the lump in my throat began to grow to the size of a basketball. I rode the Raleigh slowly back to campus and locked up my bike in the rack. There was no food in the room, but I sat up and listened to some records until after midnight. One song by the Eagles, as if to rub the school's mascot in my face with its sharp beak, had my new name on it, "Johnny come lately, there's a new kid in town … ."

"MIDNIGHT IN THE MIDWEST"
CHAPTER 2

January 2006—Midnight in the Midwest—so what if the actual event occurred an hour earlier and the only thing that we witnessed was a tape-delayed version? What difference did it make that this was replay rather than real deal? Folks like us from all across America turned on television a few minutes early in order to watch, live or recorded, because it simply would not have been the same otherwise. It was our tradition. Each year Dick Clark was welcomed into our family room to lead us counting down the final seconds. Judging from the exuberance of revelers who huddled toe-to-toe in Times Square to witness it for themselves, the gigantic Waterford Crystal ball's descent must have been a spine-tingling thrill. It even brought one or two goose bumps just to see it on TV. Sure, by the time we tuned in most of the rowdy crowd had in real life already dispersed from the scene. Even so, we pretended that all the pandemonium was being repeated over again for our benefit.

The entire evening aimed at this magical moment, and for several reasons we could hardly bear to wait any longer. First, although New York might be the city that never sleeps, it was well past our normal bedtime. Once I fantasized about standing in the midst of the mayhem at Times Square on New Year's Eve myself. No more. Middle-age and middle-of-the-night have so little in common. Second, the snacks regularly laid out around the holidays were mostly consumed. Sausage and cheese, chips and dip, even raw vegetables because something healthy was obviously required if not much desired—trays of food intended less to feed the famished than to help keep us busy. Finally, it was time. Now all the diversions designed to help us stay awake until 12 o'clock—*The War of the Worlds* on DVD, a game of spoons, even chit-chat to bring us up to date since we were together a week before on Christmas Eve—were set aside. No further need to kill time; time was slipping away all by itself. *Ten, nine, eight …* the final seconds ticked down … *seven, six, five …* partiers across the Central Time Zone paused and poised for the moment … *four, three …* the final grains of sand through the hourglass … *two, one … .* The champagne bottle was uncorked, Tammy and I kissed on the lips, and we raised our glasses in toasts with her brother and his wife. Just like we did the year before, and the year before that, and every year since they joined us living in Wisconsin. In an instant 2005 ended and 2006 was here.

Time moves on, and it was time to move on. When their kids and ours were smaller they hung around spending the night at our place rather than bundling everybody up to venture out into the cold. Those same kids had gradually grown old and clever enough to avoid being trapped inside with their parents, uncle and aunt, and Dick Clark on New Year's Eve. Much easier nowadays, therefore, to make the forty-minute drive home to West Bend and sleep in their own beds rather than toss and turn on our family room pull-out with its metal post annoyingly protruding through the thin mattress. Tired and no longer hungry, there was no point hanging around a minute more. The in-laws grabbed their wraps and relish tray and headed for the door. I followed on their heels and climbed into my Pacifica, the motor idling since the end of December so that the inside would be warmed up by the time January arrived.

Such advance planning made braving the elements a few moments later less of a chore, and I congratulated myself for preemptively getting the car started without missing a single second of Dick Clark's countdown. The distance from the house to the vehicle amounted to only a dozen or so precariously icy steps, but the trek was more bearable knowing that a reasonably comfortable place awaited me once inside the Pacifica. Thank goodness for whoever invented seat warmers. My first New Year's resolution was never again to own an automobile without this indispensable feature designed to allay the chilling effect of the frozen exterior on my leather interior. With the push of a single button my backside would be greeted with a toasty reception.

The touch of another button would bring music to my ears. As the handle was lifted and the door swung open, my favorite FM station blared over the Pacifica's deluxe car stereo with enough volume to make classic hits of the '70s audible over the defroster. Our elderly neighbors, content to welcome the New Year the next morning, would not be jarred by the sudden sound. Jumping in behind the wheel I quickly slammed the door, double-checked that the windows were rolled up tight, and backed the car out of the driveway into the Wisconsin night.

Wisconsin is the very definition of winter wonderland. As a transplant, the one thing I personally wondered most about each winter was "Why Wisconsin?" Some of the natives, I soon discovered, wondered too. It was a legitimate question, especially in January. Why would anybody not serving some kind of sentence for heinous crime actually agree to live here? Rather than leave me to shiver and curse the weather outdoors beneath my frosty breath, however, the climate-controlled environment inside the Pacifica allowed the luxury of a few minutes by myself to ruminate about other matters.

Grousing wouldn't change the situation anyway. For example, given my druthers I would have been at home and snuggly tucked under the covers for the night. Since my own warm bed was not an option, I hoped the hit songs of my youth might steer me down the proverbial memory lane while I simultaneously tracked in my mind how things were humming along in my life. If I could not enjoy the dreams of a sound sleeper, at least awake I might give conscious attention to dreams of what I wanted to accomplish the next 365 days and beyond. Winter made me wonder, but the Pacifica made it possible for me to think. Without need to wait for my brain to thaw, I also quickly warmed to thoughts of sitting even more comfortably by the fireplace and deliberately connecting those memories, dreams, and everything in between. I already had a plan for what I wanted to do.

The Roman god, Janus, for whom the first month of the year is named, was a two-headed deity with faces pointed in opposite directions. One face looked backward across time already traversed, the other glimpsed forward toward what remained ahead. The change of the calendar annually signals a unique occasion for mere mortals also to engage in retrospective reflection as well as futuristic imagination from the perspective of the here and now. New Year's created the ideal moment to do it all concurrently. This January I felt readier than usual, and my plan went beyond thoughtfully reminiscing and eagerly anticipating. I cashed in a Barnes and Noble gift certificate from Christmas on a leather-bound journal with empty pages that would soon be replete with my own prose and Janus-like perspective. The first official entry was scheduled to coincide with the first official day of the New Year.

My intention was to resume a project begun nearly nine years earlier on the eve of my election to the presidency of Concordia University. The original attempt had an unusually surprising start; I was a thirty-eight-year-old history professor who was more than a little stunned to be chosen for the position straight from the ranks of the faculty. Unfortunately, the first journal wound up being sporadic and short lived. Now, however, despite the long gap, I was motivated to write once more. Thus there followed a second resolution to accompany the one never to buy another car without seat warmers: I resolved to try again.

More specifically, I would write as a historian providing original documentary material for future historians to have a rare glimpse inside the window of someone's soul. More accurately, I would retell some of the tales of my life even at the risk that those stories might bore posterity to death. With one eye on the past and the other to the future, I would also write as a college president so that others might review parts of Concordia's history through the same lens that I used. Approaching nearly a decade in office, I figured a chapter somewhere in Concordia's saga might mention my name, so why not attempt to shape my own legacy as much as possible? Certainly, I would write about fond memories and of dreams yet to come true. More than that, I would write as a doting father so that my children would have evidence from my own hand of my fondness for them and of my intimate interest in their dreams. Finally, this time I would write as a man of faith whose struggles and successes were interpreted accordingly and whose deeply entrenched beliefs intersected and informed life at every turn. Which tests of that faith awaited not far up the road, I had no clue. For that matter I remained clueless about how to write the first page of the second iteration of my journal. The next step on a revitalized literary journey was ready to launch the following day, but page 1 needed more thought before putting pen to paper.

So I thought as I drove, turning the corner into 2006. The Pacifica might have been a tad too warm and comfortable. Splashing through the snow and slush my fatigued mind began to turn into midnight mush. I was spent. Earlier that evening, by contrast, my thoughts had soared and stretched from "Time to Eternity." That was the theme of the substitute sermon I had preached at Mount Calvary. Our pastor's gallbladder had to be removed, and thus his pulpit needed to be filled. "We are the ones to mark the passing of time," the faithful scattered in the pews heard me say, "because time is something God created for us and not for Himself. God does not live in time. God is outside of time, beyond it in eternity. He made it, and when He is done with it (when it has accomplished its intended purpose) God will put it to an end, and there will be only eternity once more."

What in Heaven was I talking about? Evidently, I was fresher just after supper than in the hour after the clock struck twelve. The point had something to do with "redeeming the time," and making the most of each moment and day while there was still time to be redeemed. That exhortation seemed a bother now. Pondering eternity any further obviously by definition could wait, and I had absolutely no inclination to redeem any more of time that day. Morning, I conceded, would be time enough to think about how best to begin recording the narrative of my personal journey in my private journal. The brain may have been thawed, but the mind was fried. Yawning, I turned up the music to enliven my senses rather than daringly resort to rolling down the window for a chilly blast and risk freezing just to remain alert. The drive, after all, would just take a couple of minutes. Only a few miles to go before I could sleep.

For the second time in one night I was on my way to church, but it was a different building in another part of town for other reasons. This trip had nothing to do with preaching, pilgrimage, or piety. The mission was more mundane. Andrew was waiting for me to fetch him from Immanuel as soon after midnight as I could get myself there. He was the middle of five children, so a middle-of-the-night pickup was fairly familiar parental duty, especially on New Year's Eve when the curfew was extended. His older brother and sister could fend for themselves while his younger sister and brother had devised other arrangements for their late night transport.

Andrew was still without a driver's license to document that a month had already passed since his sixteenth birthday. The day he would drive alone would come soon enough, and neither he nor I was in a big hurry. Andrew was occupied with other priorities, and normally I enjoyed the drop-offs and pickups because our respective schedules seldom allowed much other one-on-one time. In the Pacifica I had a captive audience and, as long as he didn't change the radio channel to hip-hop, I looked forward to being his chauffeur. That is unless the trip occurred after regular middle-age hours, which were defined by my 11 o'clock bedtime. Despite the hour, on this December turned to January winter night, Andrew was relying on me for his ride. Tonight there was no turning in until he was retrieved and returned home. I prayed he would get out of that church quickly.

There is no rest for the weary, but otherwise I should have had little cause for complaint. For one thing, I wouldn't have to trouble myself about my sixteen-year-old son sharing the road on New Year's Eve with impaired people whose friends should have confiscated their car keys. For another, parents of high school students like Tammy and me tended to worry lots less about teen parties that were chaperoned and held inside a church building.

As much as any other reason, though, it was just good for Andrew to get out of the house. We were relieved he wanted to party given how pooped he had been the previous couple of days. To be "under the weather" in Wisconsin's winter means you have to descend awfully deep, and Andrew had indeed been laid rather low. Only a few hours earlier he was nodding off in church, although by itself that need not necessarily suggest a symptom of any serious malady. Otherwise medical researchers should probably study the connection between some of my sermons and contagion. The dense remarks about "Time and Eternity" alone sent so many heads bobbing that the sanctuary should have been cordoned off for concern about the outbreak of pandemic. No need to panic, I supposed, but it was unlike him since (unlike me) Andrew never bothered much about sleep. The idea of a nap is seldom far from my mind, but Andrew was never interested in wasting time lying down when he could be up at the gym or out shooting baskets in the driveway instead. The Christmas break basketball practices must have been particularly rigorous, we concluded, or more likely Andrew had to be coming down with some virus for him to have slept as much as he had been of late.

After church he felt a little better. The hour of worship brought physical (if not spiritual) revival, or else the prospect of playing spoons with us was more than enough remedy for whatever ailed him. Andrew shook off sloth and gladly accepted the invitation to join the party at Immanuel. We agreed that he should go, as long as he was out of the church's door and in the car by 12:15, so that I wouldn't be left waiting. Andrew understood the reason for the stipulation. I wanted to get back home and go to bed, of course.

Andrew was prompt, or at least as close to on-time as I have learned to accept within our family. Rather than allow it to become a point of constant friction, I learned to acquiesce to the fact that no one inherited Billie and Eugene's good genes for punctuality, which were passed down to me. Following their mother's lead, Tammy and the kids were technically not late people, not usually. Right on time always felt more like tardy to me, but I grudgingly adjusted. Other than once causing his parents to wait up an entire frustrating night through false labor sixteen years prior, Andrew as a rule (and according to our rules) arrived when expected. As if to compensate for the false alarm while still in the womb, he was never one to cause his parents to lose sleep.

Part of the reason Andrew could be counted on was that he was fairly level headed. How could a third-born child of parents who were themselves third-born; a middle child of middle-children who was raised in a middle-class family in the Midwest be anything other than balanced? There may be something to birth order theory, or geography, or social class, but for whatever reason, Andrew was easy.

Easy, but not perfect. Most often Andrew exercised defiance by exercising, and the type of discipline that motivated him most was self-discipline. He played basketball incessantly, almost as if it were an addiction. Andrew defied his mother by staying outside perfecting his jumper even when the mercury in the thermometer dropped until there was nearly none of the red liquid left to see.

He simultaneously sought to defy Mother Nature by choosing as his passion a game best suited for freaks of nature, ones whose place on the growth charts raised the average as much as Andrew dropped it down. He was a mere 5′2″ and a scrawny 110 pounds as a high school freshman. By his sophomore year he had grown to 5′6″ and had added some weight but looked as skinny as ever—skinnier. "You have the body of a Kenyan," I regularly teased him, "and should concentrate on distance running." Once again he could follow his mother's lead. When it came to running and local road races Tammy was the one who won the prize for arriving early, ahead of the pack, and I was the straggler who showed up late. My strategy was different: I liked to start out slow—and then back off. As a runner Andrew showed promise but lacked interest. His one-track mind left little room for track or cross country. Instead he ate, drank, and slept basketball; and if sleep interfered he would stay up until long after I had retired, shooting jump shot after jump shot.

While Tammy voiced her misgivings about Andrew playing out-doors in Wisconsin's unforgiving winter, she shouldered her share of the blame for his unrepentant commitment. Andrew was very much his mother's son. For both of them self-discipline and self-sacrifice were less virtues than they were vices in which they gleefully indulged themselves. Her early years of distance running following graduation from college were kept secret from her parents because Tammy feared they would worry about the toll all the miles might take on her body. Under cover of early morning darkness she meandered through neighborhoods lit by streetlamps until her daily distance quota was reached. Later she added triathlons to her repertoire, which meant laps swimming in the pool and long rides on her bicycle to supplement her running regimen. She liked to race, but Tammy loved to win—and she often did. Being the only sister with three athletic brothers fueled her competitive instincts. Tammy was passionate about training, almost to a fault.

The same inclination to overachieve was channeled into other parts of Tammy's life alongside, though not to replace, her athletic pursuits. She was a musician who took piano lessons and occasionally played the organ at church. Tammy also was a scholar whose academic pursuits in doctoral programs were interrupted not once but twice to accommodate moves related to my career changes. What was begun at the University of Colorado in Boulder and continued at the University of Wyoming in Laramie was finally completed at the University of Wisconsin–Milwaukee. A dedicated athlete, an accomplished musician, and a freshly minted PhD, Tammy kept herself busy juggling enough things to do to have satisfied two or three active people's lives. On top of everything else, she had the rest of us to try and keep satisfied.

Our five children were born over a seven-year span. Since she was prone to morning sickness all day long throughout each of her pregnancies, battling nausea was more or less a chronic condition for a week of years. The years of family fecundity immediately coincided with her graduate study's productivity. First research and then dissertation were done with babies and toddlers in tow. Once our last child was born Tammy resumed marathon training. Amid all that she had going on in her life, including taking care of me, being a good mother was her absolute priority. Never once were her children neglected. If anything they might have assumed that Tammy was ubiquitous. None of them spent a single minute in daycare, and even babysitters were uncommon in our household. Did I mention she also had a part-time job? Andrew's mother was not Superwoman, unless, like Clark Kent, she operated incognito. There was no disguising the fact that Tammy was extraordinarily self-disciplined.

Like mother, like son. Winter, spring, summer, fall—it made no difference, every season was basketball season, and Andrew strived to perfect skills nearly every possible waking moment. Perfecting is not easy. He worked long and hard. Our elderly neighbors next door surely noticed him playing right outside their window just as I heard him out mine, but they never called to complain about the bouncing ball and rattling rim disturbing their peace and quiet. It was anything but quiet, but it was a sound that I enjoyed, and I slept more peacefully knowing that he was at home safe and sound. Tammy told me once in awhile that I snored—and I looked forward to another chance to do so as Andrew came leaping and bounding out the church and hustled toward the Pacifica, an answer to my prayer.

Who was this kid, and what did he do with my son? All of this unexpected energy caught me off guard given Andrew's earlier lethargy. I turned the radio down a notch before he got the idea to change stations and to listen to him animatedly describe his two main activities the past few hours—pickup games in the church gymnasium and consumption of an inordinate amount of junk food. Neither of these would have surprised me under normal circumstances, but I was astonished at the transformation of the early evening Andrew who had slumped in the pew at Mt. Calvary compared to the late night one who had just flown out of Immanuel.

The gap between his lively vigor and my *rigor mortis* did not escape me either. My guess was a "sugar high" and it became easier to understand his rationalization for chugging those sodas when he explained how thirsty he was from running up and down the floor. We had made a pit stop on the way home from practice the day before for the same reason—to purchase a Gatorade to help sate what seemed to be his unquenchable thirst. Leave it to Andrew to exert himself not only in practice—as a 5'6" sophomore playing varsity he had no alternative if he hoped to compete with older, taller, thicker guys—but also in a goof-around game with friends at church on New Year's Eve.

What began to concern me, as in his resurgence he continued rambling, was whether his afternoon naps and his late night soda-induced caffeine blitz had now left Andrew way too wired and not too tired to go home to bed. What if he suddenly decided to turn on the flood light over the driveway directly outside my bedroom window for a post-midnight shoot-around to compensate for practice time missed during his unscheduled afternoon siesta? What would the folks next door think this time when the ball started bouncing and the rim started rattling in the middle of the night?

If I had rolled down my window and cranked up the volume on the Pacifica's stereo at that moment the neighbors might have heard it, too: "To everything—turn, turn, turn—there is season—turn, turn,

turn—and a time to every purpose under Heaven." The lyrics to the Byrds' song borrowed from Solomon, that famous lyricist of antiquity, were playing softly on the classic hits station as we made a turn of our own into the driveway. "A time to shoot and a time to sleep," I thought to myself. Andrew showed no inclination to keep his parents awake tonight. He was home. He felt better and had fun at the party. He went to his room to turn in for the night. Perfect—Andrew made it easy for me finally to fall asleep. Tomorrow I would be fresh enough to begin a new journey, and I was going to write about it in my journal.

"MIDNIGHT MADNESS"
CHAPTER 3

October 1977—Midnight Madness—a time to play! Most programs waited until a more conventional hour later in the afternoon, after classes had ended for the day, but technically twelve o'clock on the dot on a prescribed date in mid-October marked the official time that college basketball teams were authorized to begin practice. Whose bright idea was it to hold practice in the middle of the night?

When the Byrds sang "to everything there is a season," the band's inspiration was probably not a time in mid-October when college sports fanatics would momentarily turn their frenzied attention from football to the upcoming basketball season. But, Byrd Stadium, inspired by a coach named Lefty, was the setting for college basketball's original Midnight Madness. According to legend, Lefty Driesell—men's basketball coach at the University of Maryland—began the tradition in the early '70s at the school's football venue: Byrd Stadium. The original Midnight Madness was not a media event to generate enthusiasm.

Lefty simply wanted his Terps to demonstrate their eagerness to get busy and go to work.

That first year's midnight practice session was uncomplicated: a mile run. The team ran laps around Byrd Stadium turn, turn, turning the corners of the end zone with automobile lights shining at each bend to make sure nobody cut too soon. Although there were no pep band members with painted faces performing or dance squads with bare midriffs shimmying, a few hundred Maryland Terrapin faithful got wind of the plan and showed up to support. The following year more than one thousand converged on the stadium to watch the basketball team run a midnight mile for conditioning, as most players, still rounding into form, jogged slowly in order to be sure to finish the entire distance. In 1972 the idea of adding an intrasquad scrimmage allowed eight thousand anxious Maryland partisans their first glimpse of that year's hoops team. He did not realize it at the time, but Coach Lefty Driesell launched what rapidly became an annual extravaganza and fan favorite on many college campuses. With Midnight Madness igniting the season that a few months later culminated in the fever-pitched crescendo of March Madness, college basketball fired the imagination of many young boys with hoop dreams of their own. Boys such as that other Lefty's son.

At St. John's College in October of 1977, the Midnight Madness craze had yet to permeate campus culture. Half the population of the wider Winfield metropolitan area would have had to show up to get a crowd comparable to Maryland's together. Even if there were interest, the gymnasium's rickety wooden bleachers were confined to the south side of the court. On game days when the custodian tugged them all the way out only a couple hundred people might squeeze together to sit. Why risk upsetting the fire marshall? Why trouble anyone? The sports writer from the *Winfield Daily Courier* was a one-man staff, and he would have been obliged to put in overtime to cover such an event. Rather than make any fuss, the first day of hoops practice was conducted without hoopla. Coach Ralph Skov issued each of his boys a new pair of orange Converse All-Stars and a reversible mesh jersey in school colors—black on one side, orange on the other; hauled the recently inflated basketballs out of the storage closet onto the gym's tartan surface; and blew his whistle. We were under way. As far as I was concerned, it was about time.

If not quite my *raison d'etre,* basketball was clearly my only reason for being at St. John's College. Of all of the colleges and universities in America, St. John's alone offered me a coveted athletic scholarship. The sound of it "athletic scholarship" was far more impressive than the reality. The only free ride I was getting was in the back seat of the car assuming that Lefty was unlikely to require me to kick in for gas. In fact, the financial assistance provided by the scholarship was meager, only a few hundred dollars. More important than the dollar figure, though, was the symbol. Any amount at all, as long as it was awarded as a scholarship to play basketball, was enough to massage the ego of a kid with my aspirations and ambitions. Billie may have supported my dreams, but keener and more objective observers would have immediately recognized them as delusions of grandeur. The apparent lack of interest by every coach across the country except Ralph Skov did not dissuade me, and I held to the vision that their oversight still might be corrected. Since St. John's was but a two-year junior college, I imagined taking off with the St. John's Eagles and inevitably drawing reaction from bigger college scouts bound to notice my upward trajectory. Once I was spotted, which was only a matter of time, the sky alone was the limit. That dream brought me to Winfield, and in the first few months following my arrival the delusion kept me there.

It all seemed like such a good idea when I discussed it with the Petersons. They were the source of my interest in the first place. They were also our next door neighbors, but my closeness to them went beyond the proximity of our houses. Rick Peterson was a couple of years ahead of me at Jefferson High School, where he had a solid, if not stellar, basketball career. When it came time to pick a college, Rick chose St. John's, where he enjoyed outstanding back-to-back basketball seasons. Coach Skov got my name and a flattering recommendation from Rick, and now I was following in my neighbor's footsteps. If it was good enough for Rick, I figured, St. John's was certainly good enough for me.

Rick's younger sibling, Chris, the fourth of five Peterson boys, was the brother nearest to me in age and just a grade behind me in school. He was also my best friend. As children we were inseparable whenever we were home. School days kept us apart, not so much because my class was a year in front of his, but mainly because Chris went to Bethlehem, the private Lutheran school a few miles away, while I walked a few blocks to Lumberg, the public elementary school directly across the street from Jefferson.

Once dismissed for the day, however, we were reunited for a couple of hours of unimpeded play until we saw Lefty pull into the driveway. The appearance of the Granada (or of one of its non-air conditioned predecessors) usually coincided with the church bells from the Baptist Church across the street ringing five times to indicate the hour. If his brick job was on the other side of town and Lefty got home at 5:45 we would hear the bells play a selection of gospel hymns. The tunes were unknown to me but I suspected probably familiar to Chris, though he never sang along. Lefty's arrival and the pealing carillon were my signals that Billie would soon have supper on the table and at any moment I should expect the shout summoning me to come and eat. Within minutes after dinner was devoured and the dishes were cleared I would grab the phone and dial the Petersons' number. As Chris sat beside his kitchen window and I brought up a chair next to the glassed door in our dining room, we could see each other across the yard as we spoke. Until then we had been too busy to have much of a conversation, typically too busy playing, and most often playing basketball.

According to my own admittedly biased assessment of basketball ability I was not too bad, but Chris Peterson was much better. His natural giftedness as an athlete was exceeded only by his dedication and discipline to improvement. It was never his intention to shame me, but I saw him in his backyard refining his already silky smooth shot long after I had given up on the day. I noticed him following through on free throws in foul weather that kept me confined indoors. I watched him persevering while I slipped out the front door to pursue other diversions with other friends. When he labored and I languished, pangs of conscience afflicted me. After all, we shared the same dream. Everybody knew that he was good enough to play at college basketball's highest level. Nobody knew better than I did how hard he worked to make it happen. It paid off. Chris was the best pure shooter that I or anybody from our neck of the woods had ever seen—our Colorado version of "Pistol Pete." Ever the true friend, he pretended that as a basketball player I was his equal. Once in awhile I made believe too. No one, not even Billie, urged me onward more than Chris—sometimes by his example, often through his words.

At Jefferson our paths to school finally managed to converge. Denver's Lutheran High School was distant enough from our neighborhood that once their boys completed eight years of parochial education at Bethlehem, Bill and Ardith Peterson were satisfied. In selecting a high school for their sons the Peterson parents decided Jefferson suited them just fine. At long last during my senior and his junior year Chris and I finally suited up in the red and gray, our first chance to play in the backcourt together just like we envisioned in the back yard. Our Saints' team, dominated by juniors like Chris, was a year away from being dangerous. But, even a mediocre record my last season at Jefferson could not diminish the unbridled joy I felt playing every game on the same floor with my best friend. By the time the year was over Chris had received all-state recognitions, and I was honorable mention for our conference. Other people's assessments drew conclusions not unlike my own: I was not too bad, but their accolades reinforced the truth that Chris was much, much better.

Now he could look forward to next year, when the Saints returned four experienced starters and were positioned to make a serious run at the state championship. Moreover, the college recruiting spotlight that was about to be pointed his direction was heady stuff for any kid. The future beamed bright for him, and nobody would have blamed Chris for seeing our 1977 season as a mere stepping stone toward more exciting things to come. Instead my friend was emotional when our brief play-off run abruptly and unexpectedly ended with a first round loss on the next-to-last day of the month—a February frustration that meant no March Madness for us. Jefferson's Saints would not be in that number of those marching further into the postseason. After the last game, he stayed up until two o'clock in the morning scribbling out a five-page letter. Maybe he was still being true to his school colors or, more likely, it was the only pen handy. But, the gray mood and pain his words exuded might as well have been etched with his blood as with the red ink that Chris used to write:

> I tried as hard as I could tonight to win for you and the rest, but mainly for you. I understand how much basketball means to you, this being your senior year and this is the only sport you play. You've grown up playing and have gotten better every year. In my book you're in the top three guards in the county .... Pretty soon besides being gone in basketball you'll be gone at school and not next door. I swear I'll always cherish the moments we had together, the places we went, the things we did, the people we met, and the dreams we had! Why does it have to be over?

> I asked my Mom that, and I think I'll tell you what she said. God had a reason for doing this, making our season go the way it did and all the happenings. Maybe he's testing us, but whatever it is, take it from God, for it is his will. I can't think of anything more I'd like to do right now than play our whole season over.

> I cried tonight for the first time in a long time. I think I cried for you, Pat. We're growing up so fast. Basketball is over for you in high school. I have one more year left. I cried for the thought of maybe never playing together again. I cried because you are my best friend. I cried because I wanted you to win tonight. I cried because another season is over. But, most of all I cried because you cried. No one knows what a true friend is until they have had you

.... Well its 2 o'clock. I hope I've said my part. It's all true feelings.

You'll be playing college ball sooner than you think ... .

My thought was that it would not come soon enough. The remaining weeks of my senior year buzzed by in a blur, but any ideas I might have had about a carefree summer were banished the very day after graduation. Although I lobbied for a day off before starting my summer job to celebrate the end of high school with my pals, Billie was adamantly opposed and not about to lose this argument. She reminded me that in order to cover the considerable gap between athletic scholarship and remaining tuition, every penny would count. The rest of the financial aid package and a few dollars drawn from Lefty's paychecks only went so far. If I wanted to go to St. John's College and play basketball, the message from her was both very loud and crystal clear that I had to do my share.

By six o'clock the morning after being awarded my high school diploma I was ready and reporting for duty at the road construction company where my brother Bill was a supervisor and got me work. Summer jobs, of course, have value beyond providing students with dollars that will be needed for school or other expenses. For me the most valuable lesson each summer that I worked in the paving business was the unsubtle reminder of how much I preferred going to school over manual labor. Fixing potholes and laying asphalt from sunrise to sunset five, and occasionally six days a week, made me despise summer's long days. Let the Beach Boys have their "Endless Summer"; I wanted it to be over. They were surfers; I was a sufferer, and I sought relief from summer's schedule my first day on the job.

Barely a week into that summer suffering, a glimpse of potentially better days on the horizon came my way via the U.S. Mail in the form of a newspaper clipping. An article from the Saturday, June 11th issue of the *Winfield Daily Courier* was sent to me by Coach Skov. The headline read, "St. John's Signs Basketball Duo," but my eye immediately diverted to what were obviously the yearbook-worthy senior class headshots of the two boys featured in the story. One wore a neatly coiffed Earth, Wind, and Fiery full Afro with a dark suit and tie. That contrasted with the light-colored polyester leisure suit and Bee Gees-ish feathered-cut, parted-down-the-middle hairstyle of the other. Ebony and Ivory, side by side. The first, Greg Levine, a 6'5" all-conference forward from Detroit Lutheran High School, never actually showed up in Winfield. The other, the moment he saw his picture in the paper and read about himself in the *Courier*'s sports page, couldn't wait to get there. When I finally got past the headline and picture I began to read:

> Two high school standout basketball players have signed letters of intent with St. John's College. Patrick Ferry, son of Mr. and Mrs. Eugene Ferry, Denver, Colo., has accepted a scholarship to attend St. John's this coming year. Ferry attended Jefferson High School in suburban Edgewater which plays in the Jeffco league, allegedly the toughest scoring conference in Colorado during the 1976-77 season. By averaging 12 points per game this season, he ranked among the top 20 in league scoring. He also contributed an average of 5.5 assists, 3.5 steals, and four rebounds per game. For these accomplishments and his aggressive play he was named to the all-conference team and given "top defensive player" award. Ferry is 6'1" tall and weighs 180 lbs. He had a 3.93 grade point average his senior year and graduated with a 3.6 cumulative grade … .

This first taste of small town newspaper coverage was something to savor, and the *Winfield Daily Courier* made me hungry for more.

June, however, was far from over, and the rest of summer proved to be an appetite suppressant. Sweetness turned sour. June, July, and the first part of August did not budge easily. Days dragged along. Sixty seconds a minute, sixty minutes an hour, twenty-four hours a day—the measure of time's inexorable movement is fixed and firm. One day, in spite of what it seemed, was really no longer or shorter than the next. Yet, it was as if the battery in the Timex watch Billie had given me for Christmas died, and when it stopped, time itself also stood still. Throughout the interminable day at work my wrist raised and my eyes lowered reflexively to glance at my watch in constant and repeated motion. Elusively I waited for the end of the road and the everlasting day to be over. But, there is no "end of the road" in the paving business, and while shoveling asphalt was back-breaking it was hardly mind-occupying labor. Between frequent Timex time checks there was plenty of opportunity for my mind to wander. There was more than enough time for second thoughts.

Once the thrill of seeing my name and face in print gradually waned the reality of what was about to happen slowly sunk in. Evidently Greg Levine of Detroit, Michigan, had a summer job that gave him time to rethink Kansas too. For me the hot asphalt could not prevent cold feet, as the glacial pace of time made it possible for initial excitement to turn to wariness, and for wariness to turn to dread. Dreading or not, though, and in the starkest contrast to Greg Levine, who stayed home, off to Kansas I went.

As seasons changed and summer finally became autumn, I was sorely disappointed to discover that time was unable to pick up any steam. Indeed, suffering summer's slowness was only a rehearsal for the fall semester. Paving from dawn to dusk was more like the Roadrunner speeding along through life compared to the terrible, Terrapin-like plodding of the minutes, hours, and days since Billie and Lefty dropped me in Kansas and headed back on the highway home.

She said that they ran into lots of rain but that it was a nice trip back. Stopping for lunch in Ellis, a spot in the road along I-70, and only for gas after that, Billie wrote from home that it was "550 miles from your dorm here." That was some considerable distance for folks who didn't get out much. "I wish it didn't take so long to drive it," she said, "but I'm so glad we went down and saw it all." Glad was she? Winfield unexpectedly won my mother over to the possibility that Kansas was not so bad after all. A nice place for her to visit, but then she didn't have to live there. "And, I'm sure we'll be down again," Billie continued, "Not too soon though." Not too soon? Next week might as well have been next year, the time passed so slowly.

Things were much the same at home, my mother assured, just quieter without me, my friends, and my stereo. "I feel like you are still sleeping and will be getting up soon," she went on, "and then when I look in your room it looks so empty without you and your stuff. It will take awhile to get used to your being away, but you too have to adjust to your new life and we hope it goes really well for you from here on. I'm sure it will." I didn't want to argue, but I was sure it would not. Those 550 miles might as well have been across the ocean. I couldn't swim, much less swim home. I had no Granada. Somebody sabotaged the skinny tire on the Raleigh during my first week on campus. "I'm really sorry about your bike tire and tube," she said, "there are obviously some devils at St. John's, right?" Devils maybe, hellishly hot for certain, and I was stuck there just like the hands on the Timex Billie had given me.

It struck her as a simple matter of fact that I would have to adjust to this new life of mine. Adjustment, no one could argue, is one of the basic facts of the freshmen year experience. But, my many friends in Colorado had it easier. For one thing, they were home. The territory was well known, and the commute to where they could get some of their mom's cooking or twist her arm to take care of their laundry for free was uncomplicated. Most of them were in Greeley or Fort Collins or Boulder so they didn't have to adapt to living in Kansas. Billie suspected that it would be difficult for me at first, but all I needed was a little time. "I hope you aren't homesick," she said, "because nothing much is going on here that you are missing. The first few months are the hardest. I know how I missed everyone when I went to New Hampshire. When I got back I found they hadn't missed me that much (my friends, not my family). Only because they were doing what everyone else was doing, living day to day." Besides, she was quite sure that I would be the one who benefited from striking out on my own. "In the long run you and Reed will be much more mature and better adjusted than these guys running home every week.It would be nice if you were near," she admitted, "but we think more often of you and your letters mean so much."

If letters were meaningful to Billie, they meant so much more to me. Letters were my lifeline. They linked me to the life from which I had been prematurely uprooted, and the lines that I wrote on notebook paper or read on Billie's stationery were my way of surviving life where I now was planted. Once in a while we would talk on the phone, but it was generally not worth the trouble. The pay phone nearest our room was one of only three available in the entire Rehwinkel Hall. When it rang, none of the boys within earshot hurried to answer because the odds of the call being intended for the fellow who fetched it were slim. Answering brought the added obligation of tracking down the intended recipient, which only went smoothly as long as he was in his room. Usually he wasn't and that meant scrounging for pen and paper, oddly not always immediately accessible in a college dorm room, and writing down a message from the caller. The subsequent search for scotch tape to attach the note to his door was futile, as tape was even less likely to surface amid the clutter of the room, so the message was stuffed under the door. Rather than go through the hassle, boys left the phone to ring incessantly, and we all learned to cope. It was either that or go answer yourself.

My folks didn't bother calling me unexpectedly. Instead Billie, Lefty, and I conspired upon a gangster-like plot for us to visit on the phone once a week. Too many coins were required for me to feed the pay phone for a conversation lasting more than a few minutes without the operator interrupting and requesting more. Calling collect and reversing the charges to Billie and Lefty was an option, but it was more expensive than calling direct. So I dialed "∅" and asked to place a "person to person" call to Patrick. Billie or Lefty answered innocently that Patrick was not home, and a minute later I picked up the Rehwinkel pay phone receiver with my parents, calling direct, on the line.

Such a clever system, but still it was not without flaws. Even a direct call lasting too long would overextend their budget for the phone bill. Besides, the pay phone was on the stairwell at the end of the hall in the middle of the dorm's regular traffic pattern, and there was no such thing as a private conversation. Baring your soul while boys wrapped in towels walked by on the way to the showers did not mix. Letters, on the other hand, permitted an in-depth conversation between my mother and me that went back and forth for weeks. I was not going to make the adjustment all by myself.

Letters probably made the transition lots slower, mostly by my design. I was unwilling to step out of the past long enough to give the present much time. "There is just nothing else to do," I convinced myself, "I like writing letters because then I get some back." I complained to Billie that "getting mail and falling asleep are the best parts of the day." My personal midnight madness began almost as soon as I had set foot on campus and bought stamps and envelopes in the bookstore. I wrote like a madman every free moment during the day and late into the night, pausing only to change an album on the stereo but never to answer the pay phone ringing off the hook.

Finally drifting off into sleep's ephemeral escape from Kansas, letters gave me a reason to get back up and face the next day. I would be first in line at the mail drop, peering into the little glass window of my slot and anxiously fingering through the combination to unlock and get the box opened. In the first six weeks before basketball practice started mail came for me almost every day. "The letters are really pouring in," I bragged to Billie, "I have had about 60 since coming and now average about 10 per week. I'm the envy of everybody here. These guys can't believe all my mail. I deserve it though as I write more than I get and write back the same day I get mail." "Wow!" Billie exclaimed, "What a fan club you have, also you will surely get writer's cramp."

Twenty letters in one week was the record. Among the ones in that mother lode was a letter from my mother. Of all of my correspondents, I told Billie, "You are definitely most faithful." By the end of the first semester 130 letters had appeared in my box, and twenty-eight of them were from her. No one else in the family was too reliable. Bob wrote occasionally. Bill, my mother said, was "not too good at writing and never having been away doesn't realize how much it means." Kim, she promised, was going to get at it eventually. As for Lefty, "he doesn't write to anyone so don't worry about that." But Billie vowed to "just keep pushing my pen because I want to!" I answered each one of her letters along with everyone else's. Often I penned a lengthy excursus with random ramblings that filled at least a couple of pages depending on the recipient. A five-page research paper for class was an onerous burden, but a five-page letter that elicited a reply was one way, in a way, to go home.

Writer's cramp was a legitimate concern, but Billie was more worried about my inability to relax my grip on the old days and reach out to new friends. Time, she unsuccessfully sought to persuade me, would go by quickly, "I'm really sorry you are homesick and I hope it gets better," Mom wrote, "It isn't too long until Thanksgiving and then Christmas. After that you will be busy with basketball and you will be more accustomed to your new life by then. And then it will be closer to spring and summer." In the meantime having Reed around helped. Once, however, when he was gone for the weekend visiting acquaintances in Wichita the loneliness was practically paralyzing. I told Billie that we usually were always together and without him "there is nothing to do in this town." When she mentioned that Lefty had just returned from New Hampshire and his own high school class reunion, I whined:

I'm glad Dad had a good time at his reunion. I wish we had one. I know everybody is doing their own thing but its different having only one friend around over the weekend when I'm used to about thirty. I know a lot of people here but it is not the same so don't bother trying to make me do without them. I don't want to, and I know they miss me as much as I miss them. I get about ten or more letters every week so I know.

Nevertheless, I recognized that she had a point. "Don't worry about me," I urged, "I'm just a little homesick. I know everybody misses each other because I can feel it in their letters …. I know this experience is valuable to me and I'll make it through this year." I would try to inch along through the year until at last it was next summer. Summer! Given the experience the previous few months, if summer was suddenly my goal then I understood the definition of a vicious circle, because I was in the middle of one myself. The vicious shrinking of my social circle tightened like a noose. Only old friends with access to paper and pens, stamps and envelopes could extricate me.

My state of mind in the state of Kansas was only part of the struggle to adjust to my new surroundings. Winfield was also hard on my body. The invitation to make some cash hauling hay was a disaster from the beginning, and I should have known better. Before I bucked even a dozen bales I broke out in an allergic reaction that brought my agricultural career to a halt in less than a half hour. A long hot shower and a dose of the allergy medicine that Billie had sent along "just in case" opened my clogged sinus passages, and the rashes were gone in a day or two.

As the hay fever subsided, a more disconcerting problem arose. First-year students like us were warned to watch out for a lifestyle and diet that could result in adding the infamous "freshman fifteen" extra pounds. Bev Lessing told Billie that Reed had actually dropped weight during his first two weeks on campus, and my mom wondered how I was doing with cafeteria food. Since she always denigrated her own cooking, Billie imagined that St. John's cuisine would be a welcome upgrade. "You mentioned that you heard Reed lost five pounds," I replied, "to date, I have lost 23 lbs. from 185-162." I never missed breakfast (except when they served that stuff on a shingle), lunch, or dinner and consumed "a ton of food at each meal." The blame, I suspected, was due to the combination of beastly heat and humidity and the unprecedented intensity of my own preseason regimen of practice to get ready for middle October. Not to fret, though, I reported that I was stronger than ever, faster than ever, and not just skinnier than ever.

Telling Billie not to worry, however, was to ask her or most any normal mother to ignore maternal instinct. If Lefty lapsed in his tendency to drive Billie crazy, Lord knows my wide range of mental and physical maladjustments over a mere month and a half should surely have driven the woman mad herself. And, as if these were not enough, the mind and body struggles collided in a perfect storm with a Kansas-like tornadic turbulence beginning to twist and turn within the depths of my spirit.

The rigor of college course work was an adjustment for most kids. Independence brought opportunities for an after-hours social life that competed with a good night's sleep and curtailed time spent in the library to prepare for class. Courses at St. John's were not bereft of challenge, but the adjustment to them went beyond having to study harder than I did in high school. The classes themselves were peculiar. The professors who taught them were peculiar. I wrote home to Billie and Lefty that we were reading Homer's *Iliad* in world literature— nothing unusual about that class. Mr. Jensen at Jefferson High might have been a more entertaining English teacher than Professor Skov, but Ralph was also Coach Skov, so I was motivated to try to impress. "I'm writing this during world lit. to avoid falling asleep," I said in a letter to my little sister, "This is Coach Skov's class so every now and then I look up to look like I know what's going on."

Psychology, on the other hand, struck me immediately as especially peculiar. At Jefferson one of my favorite subjects senior year was psychology, and I looked forward to more in-depth study of the mysteries of human motivation and behavior. In my very first missive home I indicated how I was thrown off by St. John's Professor John Saleska's approach:

Dear folks,

I just received your letter. We are through with the first day of classes and so I will just study this afternoon. I also need to buy some more books so the full bill is not yet complete. The courses I went through today carry extremely distinct religious overtones. I hope to do well in all subjects yet the way they are taught, the philosophies expressed, and the opinions represented are all quite foreign to me. Psychology in particular, it seems. It appears that while similar, Christian Psychology and the Psychology I'm used to have many differences. For instance we begin each Psych class with a student-offered prayer. I believe I'll pass. I would like you to send my notes from high school, particularly in Psychology ....

Professor Saleska was the most popular teacher at St. John's. His sense of humor was on display every Monday, Wednesday, and Friday morning. He began our first-hour class with a monologue rivaling the ones I watched Johnny Carson perform the night before if reception was good enough to pick up the Wichita station on Reed's black and white television. His comedic shtick, however, was not his main claim to fame. Everybody said that he had the Bible memorized, and I believed it when I heard him quoting all kinds of passages to reinforce whatever points he was making. At least I assumed they were Bible passages. I didn't know Homer from Hebrews or the *Iliad* from the Acts of the Apostles—it was all Greek to me. I couldn't help but like him. He enjoyed teaching in a subject area that interested me. He also gave the impression that he was a basketball fan and often inquired about the team. Professor Saleska was hilarious, and he might have had a career in stand-up had he listened to his alter ego. Nevertheless, I was more interested in superego, and ego, and id. In my high school-educated opinion his unabashed willingness to teach psychology as the "study of the soul" based on the Bible rather than Freud was fraud. I told Billie, "I've been in some pretty heavy debates about Christian influences in Psychology and Sociology classes. Sure, there is some religious influence, but it is not absolute as suggested in these classes. Fortunately, I am up on these topics and spoke well on my views."

She could counsel me to take my homesickness one slow day at a time. She could advise me to eat plenty of salty food and drink lots of water to curb my weight loss. But, when it came to the matter of how to deal with spirituality Billie left me pretty much to my own devices. It was, after all, a topic that we avoided religiously in our family. But, it was unavoidable at St. John's. Billie wrote, "I'm sure all the religion will not affect your own personal feelings or judgment. You either have need for it or you don't, and it seems some need it more than others. Just be objective about it all. Turn it off when you've had enough." If only I knew where to locate the switch.

This problem would never have happened at Jefferson High School. Rick Peterson's Lutheran grade school years must have made it easier for him to adjust to the overt religious ethos of St. John's College. I was determined to resist. Nobody, no matter how shrewd, would dupe me into taking all this Lutheran stuff too seriously. My antenna was up, and if I could not pick up a good FM station on my stereo, or every network on Reed's television, at least I would be on guard against anybody who might try to mess with my mind, or worse, try to save my soul.

Looking around, I judged that the students sitting beside me in English or psychology class, or those who sat at the same table for meals in the Campus Center must be peculiar, too, except maybe for Reed and possibly a few other athletes on campus. The rest I suspected were probably life-long Lutherans or even preachers' kids like Rev. John Rolf's daughter, Laura, from my hometown. Unlike me and the Petersons she went to Denver Lutheran High School, not Jefferson. Whether some of them were bicycle vandals masquerading as saints or the genuine article, I did not want to be in their number.

The only saints I cared to know were Jefferson Saints, and those friends were back at home, not at St. John's. Staying in touch with them from a distance would be the only social interaction I cared to pursue my first months on campus. So what if they were 550 miles away—I would lean on them.

"Lean on me, when you're not strong, and I'll be your friend. I'll help you carry on ...."

In the summer of 1972, Bill Withers' hit reached #1 in the charts. Five years later it was theme music for my freshman year. We were told that a Johnnie named Paul Hill actually authored the song "Lean on Me" a few years before it became popular while he was a student at St. John's College. Rumor was he wrote the lyrics in the basement of Rehwinkel Hall. "So just call on me brother, when you need a hand … just call me." Hopefully, somebody on the floor would answer the phone. I preferred to lean on my friends through letters, lots and lots of letters.

The only way that I averted going mad myself was the reminder of why I came to the "City of Trees" in the first place. It was time to tune out the religion and turn my attention to the basketball season. Turn, turn, turn—the rest was for the birds.

"MINUTES BEFORE MIDNIGHT"
CHAPTER 4

January 2006–March 2007 —(with a brief interlude in July 1997)
A few minutes before midnight on January 1, 2006—my intention had
been to get to the task much earlier in the day, sometime between the
Rose Parade and the full slate of college football. In fact, I never actually
watched the Tournament of Roses festivities and seldom paid much
attention to the bowl games. My preference was to do almost nothing
at all. New Year's Day offered the rare chance to sleep late then lounge
around in sweatpants, a long-sleeved t-shirt, and slippers until it was
bedtime again. To find an hour or so during such a lazy day should
have been easy enough. Procrastination certainly had potential to cause
a delay. However, merely putting it off does not account for what took
me so long finally to sit down and start writing the journal. Rather, the
first page of the journal itself explains:

Not exactly what I had in mind. Yes, I intended to restart journal writing today—nearly nine years since my last entry during the first year of my presidency at Concordia. But, I thought my initial entry would be different than it will be. Actually, I have been thinking about what I wanted to do. In addition to recounting daily things, I plan to do some retrospection and draw upon some moments in my past that I want to record. I probably will still do that but the events of the day demand attention.

Interestingly, I began my last experiment in journaling on the eve of my election to Concordia's presidency, and all of the days that followed were touched by that event. My hope and prayer is that today's events will not have the same sort of shaping impact … .

I knew that nothing would quite match the fortuitous beginning of my first attempt at recorded self-reflection on July 1, 1997. That story was one that I would never forget. "Today seemed like a good day to begin a journal," I wrote on the first page at my initial foray into journal writing nearly a decade before. A week prior to starting to write back then I had been encouraged by Pastor Elmer Neitzel, our eminent pastor emeritus at Mount Calvary, to keep a diary. I was humbled that this distinguished gentleman who was nearing the end of his own eventful life's journey thought mine was interesting enough that I should preserve an account. What better time to commence? "Today is the last chapter of one part of our lives, and tomorrow begins a new one."

No, I was not privy to confidential information about how the next day's presidential election at Concordia would go. Rather, I knew that either I would be chosen or, more likely, I would accept an offer to become vice president of academics at a smaller sister institution in Austin, Texas. Which of the two possibilities would ultimately occur seemed obvious as far as I was concerned. In fact, our Milwaukee home was already sold in anticipation of the move to Texas. Tammy and I had applied to enroll our children in school and were working with a Realtor in Austin. A letter of acceptance of the vice presidency was written and in an envelope with stamp affixed and set to drop in the mailbox. Pausing for the outcome of Concordia's election before ordering our affairs was not a luxury we could afford since I was scheduled to depart the same day for a two-week teaching stint in Tallin, Estonia. The best I could hope for was to get word of the electors' decision before my flight left Milwaukee.

"My feeling is that another will be chosen," I said not so much to appear self-effacing as in recognition of the fact that I had just turned thirty-eight years old and had absolutely no higher education administrative experience. About all that I brought for credentials was the rank of assistant professor of history with six years of teaching under my belt—a wispy thin résumé that would have trouble holding up through the interview process. Not much, but no matter. The call to move somewhere close to the Austin City Limits sounded lovely and escaping Wisconsin's winters was more than a little inviting. We gave our snow blower to my brother-in-law as a parting gift. Tammy shared my enthusiasm about Texas, as did the children "except for Andrew," I wrote, who at that time was age seven. He schemed about hiding somewhere to avoid our imminent departure.

Of course, the vacant college presidency for which I was shockingly one of five finalists had to be filled first. With nothing to lose, I sought to make a positive impression by being well prepared for the evening interview on campus. Part of that preparation for me included a study of St. Paul's letters to the young pastor Timothy. The Apostle assured his protégé that he did not receive a cowardly spirit, but a spirit of power, love, and good judgment. I prayed that a double measure of that spirit would rest on me. It also seemed prudent to advise the electors of Paul's exhortation to Timothy, "Let no one look down on you because of your youth …." When we met I reminded them that Martin Luther King was younger than I was when he gave his famous "I Have a Dream" speech, and—even more compelling for my interviewers— Martin Luther himself had yet to reach my age when he stood before the Holy Roman Emperor and courageously stated, "Here I stand, I can do no other, so help me God." Good material, I figured, but not likely good enough. By day's end I reflected, "The interview went very well. However, my sense remains that I will not be chosen …. A great run today—8 miles in muggy, sultry weather. Tomorrow promises to be quite a day." First it would be preceded by quite a night.

The heat and humidity at mid-afternoon was precursor to terrific storms in the middle of the night. The room lit up from lightning bolts, and the house shook with the thunder's clatter. The weather became severe enough that our middle child sought security and crawled into bed to sleep between his parents. This was the same fellow who was willing to strike out on his own rather than move with his family to Texas? We awakened to find the basement flooded, and our morning was spent heaving ruined carpet out to the curb for disposal and then disinfecting the rest of the mess downstairs. By noon the unwelcome chore was mostly finished and we ate our peanut butter and jelly sandwiches as we nervously waited for the phone to ring.

An hour later, a call came from a friend on campus who forwarded the rumor "from a very reliable source" that the electors were locked up between two candidates, neither of them me, and might be cloistered for some time. I returned to the couch to resume reading a book to little Andrew, who was fully recovered from the harrowing storms the night before but now was distraught by the inside scoop just received. It appeared his plan to hide at some undisclosed Wisconsin location rather than move to Texas was about to become necessary. More relief than disappointment was my reaction, but I still held out hope that there would be official confirmation of the result before my ride to the airport arrived. No sooner had I sat down than the phone rang again and the chair of Concordia's board said to me, "Pat, congratulations!"

The next ninety minutes bustled with activity as word trickled out and well-wishers rushed to make contact. Finally scrambling out the door to catch my plane, I embraced the kids, kissed Tammy good-bye and charged her with the duty of finding us a new house—preferably one with a basement that would not leak. The all-night flight to Europe was smooth, but turbulence inside me began to churn until it left me practically shaking in my seat in fear. Now I was the one who wanted to run away and hide. With nowhere else to turn, I crawled to my Father, seeking comfort through prayer, but I did not sleep one wink.

Fast forward once again to New Year's Day, 2006:

> Interestingly, I began my last experiment in journaling on the eve of my election to Concordia's presidency, and all of the days that followed were touched by that event. My hope and prayer is that today's events will not have the same sort of shaping impact— though it is clear that Andrew's life has been dramatically touched and changed.

> I finally sat down to write after I kissed my son "good night" at the end of a long and difficult day. Only a few hours earlier, we were in the

emergency room at Children's Hospital where Andrew, just a month past his sixteenth birthday, was diagnosed with type 1 diabetes.

The clarity of the symptoms was painfully obvious in retrospect. "Probably a virus," we erringly supposed over the previous days leading up to New Year's. Fatigue—all of those naps during the Christmas break would not have caused me to bat an eye had it been anybody other than Andrew stealing extra sleep. He struggled to drag himself out of bed and down the stairs; but I was slow to react. Thirst—constant "bubbler breaks" at basketball practices, not to avoid wind sprints but just to relieve his parched throat. Gatorade at the gas station, soda at the party, scrounging around the refrigerator for more beverages in an insatiable quest to quench; it should have been a signal. Weight loss— wearing his jeans low with his boxers showing was in vogue, but he looked emaciated and malnourished because, almost before our eyes, he dropped fifteen pounds from his already slight and slender body. At last check, he weighed in at 125, but now stepping on the scale he nudged the needle so that it barely touched 110; "skinnier than ever" was not just our imagination. Dizziness, frequent urination, and every other red flag that merited notice much sooner finally convinced us to call a nurse. She said it could wait until the next day, but we decided we had delayed too long already and a trip around the corner to the twenty-four-hour clinic was quickly arranged.

The doctor doing holiday duty took a blood test. When he returned after only a few minutes his instruction was for us to go to Children's Hospital right away. Andrew's blood sugar count exceeded what the meters at the clinic were capable of reading. There was no doubt in his mind, but the doctor left it to the hospital to confirm the diagnosis.

The short drive to the hospital was like a trip through a dark tunnel leading to an unknown and worrisome destination. Whatever the extent of my unfamiliarity about diabetes, it was immediately evident that Andrew knew far less. Would he still be able to play basketball? The question he asked out loud had already crossed my mind. At that moment basketball was not first on my list of concerns, though it ranked high on Andrew's. All I could say was that this was pretty serious, but it was better to wait and hear what the doctors told us.

For the rest of the ride we made feeble attempts at humor to lighten the gloomy situation. Care was taken to avoid kidding too much and going out of bounds. Except we had no idea what the boundaries now were—all of a sudden the lines were redrawn. Despite whatever exterior of calm each of us pretended to the other, beneath the surface there was concern about all that this might mean. We parked the Pacifica and walked briskly toward the sliding glass doors. The staff was waiting for us. Diabetes, we quickly discovered, was serious enough to allow us to jump ahead of others in the waiting area whose emergencies were judged less urgent. An empty bed was made available and the curtain was drawn for privacy to allow Andrew to change. He slipped out of blue jeans that were already drooping halfway down his hips and into a hospital gown. The medical team set into motion another series of blood tests. Their results would be no surprise but would merely corroborate what we suspected. The bigger question was "what now?"

Rather than pass the next few hours with uninformed banter or uncomfortable small talk, we turned on the television, checked on football scores, and wound up getting hooked on a movie. *Vertical Limit* is a thriller about an expedition to reach the summit of K2, one of the highest mountains in the world, and an arduous and dangerous climb. Literally a cliff-hanger, the plot had more than enough excitement to distract us while doctors and nurses alternated interruptions with their barrage of pokes and pricks that left Andrew looking like a pin cushion. Sitting out of the way in a soft chair in the corner I processed and I prayed.

Prior to this evening, I had measured Andrew's "vertical limits" by having him stand straight and not so tall beside the door frame and marking with a pencil his agonizingly slow growth. He stood at sixty-six inches and counting, but not counting fast or far enough for either him or me. Now complaints about his height seemed shallow. For a basketball player being vertically challenged was tough but not insurmountable. All at once Andrew faced a more difficult and daunting metaphorical mountain. As you climb, your perspective inevitably changes. Diabetes was a New Year's night wake-up call to review what really mattered. The plot to how this would play out required undivided attention, and over the next several days the Sherpa staff members at Children's Hospital would expertly guide us along treacherous paths that were completely unknown to us but that they had traveled with others before.

The normal range for a person's blood glucose level is 75–120. Anything higher than that number is cause for concern, as many millions of Americans who suffer from type 2 diabetes have discovered. Type 2 diabetics generally treat their malady through a moderation of diet, added exercise, and some medication in an effort to forestall the long-term effects of elevated blood sugar levels.

The tests run at Children's Hospital showed Andrew's blood glucose level at exceeding 1,100—"a lab legend!" according to one of the assistants doing evening rounds. Type 1 diabetes, once known as "juvenile diabetes" because it so often afflicted children like Andrew, is far less prominent than type 2. Only 10% of diabetics suffer the type 1 variety, and what distinguishes them is that they are entirely insulin dependent. The pancreas fails completely to produce insulin, which means type 1 diabetics must calculate for themselves the correct amount to inject depending on carefully watched blood sugar levels as well as specific carbohydrate intake for meals and snacks. Exercise and other activity also have an effect on glucose levels in the blood, and insulin doses have to be adjusted accordingly. Too much insulin, and blood sugar levels could fall low enough to send the diabetic into insulin shock. Not enough insulin increases the risk of ketoacidosis or toxic acids infiltrating the bloodstream with an ugly array of side effects. In between the two extremes are the lows and highs that are the common scourge of every diabetic. Low blood sugar counts cause dizziness or shaking and require the diabetic to halt even the least physical exertion and to ingest fast-acting sugars or risk passing out, while high counts cause discomforts like nausea or headaches, which, if untreated, have long-term erosive effects on the body. Here was the dramatic change touching and permanently reshaping Andrew's life and, at least temporarily, also mine.

As midnight finally struck, I finished writing the January 1, 2006, entry in my journal:

> Time to go to bed. I am suffering with a head cold—couldn't hear out of one ear last night preaching at Mount Calvary's New Year's Eve service (Pastor Eggebrecht had his gall bladder removed and was in need of a substitute). I guess compared to diabetes and a gall bladder removal, a little cold is kind of minor. I preached on 'Time and Eternity.' Sickness and weakness, and the change of the year remind me of the shortness of life and the limits of time.

Thanks be to God for the promise and the gift of eternal life that is ours in Christ Jesus.

What a difference a day made. On New Year's Eve, as I had motored along in my warm Pacifica, I was unmoved by my own message. Time and eternity suddenly became much more relevant over the next twenty-four short hours.

What a difference two more days made as Andrew put on his Milwaukee Lutheran uniform to return to the basketball floor. This answered his question about ever playing again. It also marked the introduction of the "go bag" which he carried over his shoulder out of the locker room and inconspicuously slid under the bench. The "go bag" was an accessory not for fashion but for function—carrying supplies that might be needed to moderate blood sugar levels. The bag was stocked with lances to poke his fingers, test strips on which to apply drops of blood, and a glucose meter into which the strips were inserted to generate readings. Glucose tablets and juice boxes for quick bursts of sugar were in the bag in case he dipped too low, and a supply of insulin was available in case he went too high.

Before ever leaving the house for the gym the dosage of insulin for his pre-game meal had to be modified in recognition that he would soon be vigorously exercising. A blood sugar check toward the end of warm-ups after he worked up a sweat indicated whether his count was high enough to compete safely. Once the game started and adrenaline kicked in, the blood sugar level might rapidly increase. In the hours after the final buzzer he had to be on guard against dropping too low as the adrenaline subsided. Until his count reached an acceptable point of 100 and rising, Andrew had to keep himself awake and check every fifteen minutes. If there was any lingering doubt, the alarm was set to arouse him to draw blood and run a test in the middle of the night. Basketball games now had to be fitted into this regimen.

The first game back, this routine was new and unrehearsed. Andrew was a little tentative and looked a bit ragged, but considering all he had been through it was a remarkable feat. I was impressed by his grit and proud of his determination. News travels fast within a high school community, and the steady stream of people promising their prayers and offering their support was welcome, though it made it hard to concentrate on the game. As difficult as it was for me, it was far more complicated for Andrew. While his teammates grabbed for sugar-laden Gatorade during a thirty-second timeout, Andrew abstained. During a full timeout he'd quickly poke a soon-to-become calloused finger for a fresh drop of blood and run a quick check on his meter to ensure that he was in range. In between, God only knows what had to be running through my son's mind. Keeping his head in the game could not compromise the necessity of keeping his body safe and blood sugar under control.

A three-point specialist from all those hours practicing jumpers in the driveway, Andrew was accustomed to taking his share of shots on the floor. Now he had to get used to taking shots on the sidelines in order to stay in the game. "I am rooting for Andrew in a different way now compared to before Christmas," I wrote, "Sure, I still want him to succeed. Now, however, I am thankful that he is able to participate." The way things look to you changes on the way up the mountain.

As part of the diabetes drill, a new halftime strategy was implemented. Before joining his teammates in the locker room to hear the coach's speech Andrew met me in the training room. He did a blood sugar check, and we strategized about necessary interventions before he returned to the court. This pattern became standard operating procedure for the rest of his sophomore season. At first Tammy and I were on needles and pins of our own, scoping his every fidget and wiggle with focused intensity to be sure that he was doing all right. Andrew appreciated the assistance. After a while, though, being diabetic became sort of a "new normal," and he was capable of managing fine without me. We kept meeting at the break anyway as a precaution. Better safe than sorry.

Gradually our brief halftime conversations became less about diabetes and more about game analysis—how many fathers wouldn't love a chance to offer a little basketball advice at halftime? No doubt many would be only too happy to get in the ear of his kid, or the coach, or the ref, but only the raving lunatics actually left their seats during the game except to get popcorn. Security kept an eye on those guys. Nobody ever thought to restrain me because my lunacy was kept secret.

Never did I dare to berate a referee from the grandstands. Not once did I ever complain to a coach about my kid's playing time. True, Andrew and his siblings were subjected to a little of my armchair quarterbacking at home, but I was generally careful not to overdo the father/coach bit. Nevertheless, my preoccupation was slowly but perceptibly returning to my own old normal—I began worrying less about how diabetes might drag Andrew down and resumed wondering more about how far basketball might carry him forward. Almost as soon as he learned to dribble a basketball this question started bouncing around in my mind. A diagnosis of diabetes reformed my priorities, but not entirely and not for long. Now that the crisis reached a plateau, I fell into a familiar rut that proved difficult to escape.

The end of the sophomore year was itself a halftime of sorts—

Andrew was halfway through his high school basketball career at Milwaukee Lutheran. The first two years were merely prologue; it was during the second half that the stakes got higher and the game became more compelling. Andrew could be trusted to do everything within his capacity to get himself ready. The night after his sophomore season wrapped up in late February I watched him out the window working on his game at ten o'clock in subfreezing temperatures. There was nothing unusual about his behavior; nights off would have been more likely to get the neighbors' attention. This, however, marked the beginning of the pivotal period. I took note: "Next year will be interesting—especially as he gets a better handle on his diabetes. He is outside now and even though it is 20 degrees he's working on his shooting. He does it every night. Nobody deserves success more than Andrew." That had become my mantra: nobody deserved success more than Andrew. For my part, a full-court parental press during the second half was not my style, but I was set to dish out any assists that I could to support Andrew's quest to test his vertical limits. My mind worked overtime on how to help.

A few months after Andrew's diagnosis of diabetes I noticed the symptoms of what had become my own obsessive-compulsive abnormal normal. That was my diagnosis of me. A simple blood test led to confirmation of Andrew's condition. Only a little self-awareness was required for me to recognize that I put an enormous emphasis on Andrew's basketball and, as enjoyable as it was, it was also troubling. "My emotional investment and personal involvement is way too high—even unhealthy," I lamented. "Instead of just watching him play and enjoying the observation of him being involved in the game that he loves, I note and analyze every detail from performance, to statistics, to psychology ... I am truly a case."

We tried to give our children broader exposure to many things as they were growing up—drama, music, travel—but as we moved along, our passions returned again and again to sports. "We pay lots less attention to their marks in school (which are generally pretty good) than to their points per game ... ." Not an easy admission for an academic. "From sire to son the bane descends," rued the hymn writer regarding the fall of our first parents in paradise and the unhappy inheritance handed on to subsequent generations. Tracing my problem all the way to Adam was a bit of a reach, but clearly the apple did not fall far from the tree. Eugene's genes were inescapable, and Andrew's lineage was unmistakable. The glucose meter might not detect it, but basketball was in Andrew's blood.

What astounded me even more, however, were his uncanny resemblances to the one who was almost like a brother to me. The ball bouncing and rim rattling during those lonely late nights in the backyard echoed similar sounds from years before, and Andrew's "nothing but net" sweet shot conjured images in my mind of my best friend, Chris Peterson. Was history repeating itself, or was I hallucinating? Of course, it was neither history nor psychology. It was simpler: nobody deserved success more than Chris Peterson, nobody except Andrew. Maybe my son could achieve as a basketball player what his father's friend had accomplished, and what his father had not.

His dream was to play Division I college basketball, and it was no more complicated than that. Lots of young boys imagine the same thing, but along the way they adjust their goals in order to bring them into closer conformity with reality. I had the same aspiration once.

Andrew was willing to expend perspiration to make dream and reality blend into one.

During the summer before his junior year there were certainly moments. Flashes of genuine potential and examples of exceptional performance made me think his goal was not entirely unattainable. There were also reality checks. He deserved success if hard work was the key, but there are definitely no guarantees. Competition against some of the best high school players in the country raised questions about whether his aims were too lofty. His lack of physical maturity was one issue. "And lest we forget," I wrote, "there is diabetes. No wonder I root for him. No wonder I encourage him. But, I also need to help him manage expectations without raining on his parade." The summer before his junior year had its ups and downs.

What goes up must come down; there is a certain immutability of the law of gravity. Ups and downs were part of Andrew's diabetic reality, but he learned to handle the inevitable highs and lows associated with his condition. "Gravity," as in serious business, however, was hardly a word to associate with summer basketball. That did not stop me from taking the AAU schedule very seriously, and I watched as if Andrew's entire future rested on every game. His highs on the basketball floor brought elation, while his lows caused disproportionate angst. At the conclusion of one evening practice session, Andrew dazzled his teammates by connecting on a jaw-dropping forty-four consecutive three-point shots. If evidence was needed to vindicate my assertion that the kid could shoot, there were witnesses to this remarkable demonstration. I was fully prepared to summon them if necessary. Three days later in a meaningless game, his shot was off, making me moody and provoking harsh comments that I later regretted:

I cannot understand why I live and die so much with him and his basketball. It is not healthy, really. I tend to be Andrew's severest critic. Of all that he has had to overcome to be a successful basketball player—smallness in stature, diabetes, etc.—maybe the biggest obstacle is me. I should draw back and let him find his way on his own. He may or may not go just as far either way. But, I bet it will be a whole lot more fun for him if I am out of the mix. It will probably be less stressful for me, too. But, I can't figure out how to detach, and I'm not sure that I would even if I could.

I could not. Two weeks later, after another cold shooting performance, I again berated myself for faulty priorities and flawed preoccupations and searched for simply being supportive of Andrew's interests and dreams. "But, I need to let them be his dreams that he pursues." His largeness of heart could overcome smallness in size or a pancreas that did not function. My own heart may have been in the right place, but my brain kept getting in the way. I was weary of over-analysis, and my proclivity to assess every physical or even metaphysical explanation for a bad game had become irksome to me. "Why am I wired in such a way that I cannot step back from this?" I asked myself. I had a theory:

> I cannot escape the thought that maybe I am trying to live out my own 'once upon a time' dreams through Andrew. I came up way short of my goals. He has more potential to reach farther, and I am eager to help push. He doesn't need much pushing. Andrew has dreams of his own and pursues them with vigor. I'd like to think that I want him to be successful so much because he wants it so much.

I would not have been the first father ever to be accused of trying to relive his not-so-glorious glory days through his child. That, however, did not make me any less pathetic. To my credit, I at least recognized that I spent an inordinate amount of time thinking and praying about the subject—including reflection on my own motives. The journal that I began the first day of the year made this abundantly clear as time went by: "If these pages are supposed to be an honest account and open window into me at this moment, it is fair to read and know that this consumes lots of energy and attention." Whether I was "over the top" was subject for debate. Other people and priorities were not being short-changed. But, I wrote that it was "fair to ask whether or not I have the right perspective on all of this." That was what I sought and prayed for—to approach the whole thing in the best and most helpful way that I could.

My summer struggle had some relief once the AAU mercifully ended, though I marked my calendar for the recurrence that I already anticipated the following year. Unfortunately, the relapse didn't wait until then—the first months of his junior year's basketball season pushed me closer to the point of utter irrationality. Before the season, there were high expectations for Andrew's contribution, but after a few games the marginalized role to which he was being relegated came as a huge shock. "This would not have been our expectation starting out," I observed, "but I am quickly trying to modify my outlook." I challenged myself to examine things from a new angle:

> In particular I am seeking perspective and an ability to look at the situation from a better point of view. Obsession is foolish, frustration makes no sense. This is supposed to be a game. It is meant to be fun. I hope that I can begin to approach the whole thing more reasonably and responsibly.

Indeed, I have been challenged by this in a rather profound way.…

How much more would I prefer to approach this piously, insightfully, supportively, humbly—not just because it would benefit Andrew, but because it is the right thing to do.

On the day before his late November birthday and amid the confusion regarding his role on the squad, one thing, I said to myself, was clear, "I am grateful to have him for a son. He is my hero, my inspiration, and I will always be his biggest fan—no matter what." Later that evening Andrew was used sparingly and went scoreless for the first time in my recollection. He was in a funk, and I was working hard to avoid one:

> I am trying to learn what I can from this experience—about myself. It is not as theological as I have been making it out to be. There are not cosmic consequences attached to each game. What disturbs me is how much it disturbs me. Is there some way to disconnect myself from this? I would prefer, I think, to be totally removed and uncaring rather than in my current mental state. The bigger question is how can I be of most help and support to Andrew? This is about him and not about me. Here is my chance—he has just pulled in the driveway. God help me!

He wasn't ready to talk, so I took a brisk walk and then came home to record my impressions. I wrote about how being a man is not determined by athletic prowess. I did not want Andrew to have that impression. Sport can teach us so much about respecting our teammates and striving together. "Too often," I observed, "we take away other lessons." I did not want my son to suppose that my love for him or pride in him was in any way attached to his skill or performance.

Raising him was not a project based on a couple of games, or even a season, but his whole life. Ultimately, success would measured by what kind of man he turned out to be. What kind of husband? What kind of father? What kind of son? What kind of brother? What kind of friend? What kind of person? "If this was not what basketball was helping teach Andrew," I insisted, "then maybe he was wasting his time." When I finished writing I felt like maybe there was hope for me after all!

At least I was asking some of the right questions, but that did not free me from bouts of repeated anguish. It got a little worse before it got better: "Either the situation has become crazy or maybe just I have gone crazy—and Tammy along with me," I wrote as Christmas break neared. While I steadfastly refused to complain to his coach about Andrew's paucity of playing time I vented to my friend, Paul Bahr, Milwaukee Lutheran's school principal, as we stood together along the baseline of a December home game. Mr. Bahr is a grizzled veteran administrator who has heard it all before. My slightly veiled threats to explore other school options for Andrew did not unsettle him. He knew me too well to suppose I would consider moving a kid of mine out of a Lutheran school. Still, he listened patiently and allowed me a chance to let off some steam. Maybe he was surprised to hear some of this kind of stuff from me, or maybe not. Either way, it was not the first time in his career that he'd had to deal with a lunatic parent.

Misery, I discovered, also loved company. Most every other father and a fair share of mothers in the crowd with sons on the team felt much the same way that I did to one degree or another. Bottom line, each one of us wanted his or her boy, whatever his particular role on the team or however deep he was buried on the bench, to play. Preferably to play more, and when he was in the game to be the recipient of the pass when he eluded his defender, and to take the shot when there was an open look, and to stay on the floor when the next substitute checked in. The way that individual parents expressed frustration varied. Most of the grumbling was under our breath, but occasionally the dissatisfaction was more palpable and the tension was thick.

I derived a twisted sort of consolation that my friend, Jim Barnett, father of Andrew's best friend Jake, was more miserable than I was. Like Andrew, Jake was a junior. However, he attended Wauwatosa East High School, near where his mother and stepfather lived. Jake's older brother went to Milwaukee Lutheran, but the Barnett's never felt like their eldest son got the treatment—or playing time—that he deserved. Jim Barnett and his ex-wife Sandy did not agree about many things, but they concurred that Jake would go elsewhere to high school. Besides, Wauwatosa East was renowned for its successful basketball program and for its near legendary coach, George Haas. Jake and Andrew, not unlike my best friend Chris and me, had much the same dream but would not have the opportunity to pursue it as teammates. Jim was convinced Jake's full potential had the best chance of being reached at Wauwatosa East. Unfortunately, it did not appear to be working out as planned, as Jake was seeing limited varsity action early in his junior year. Jim Barnett was fit to be tied—with a straight jacket. I feared for his, and for Coach George Haas' safety!

If Paul Bahr was willing to provide a listening ear to my irrational rants, then I figured I could do as much for Jim. The more I listened to him, however, the more I recognized an only slightly exaggerated version of myself. It was like glancing into one of those mirrors at an amusement park that distorts your reflection a little bit, but there is no mistaking who the caricature represents. Looking at Jim Barnett's situation from his point of view, I saw a minimally modified model of my own. Listening to his perception of the circumstances he experienced, I heard the echo of my own voice, which was only a little more muted. I felt sorry for Jim Barnett, but mainly I was feeling sorry for myself:

> Jake Barnett, Andrew's friend is struggling. His Dad, Jim, struggles even more. Jim just called and we talked for half an hour about how bad the situation is for Jake at Wauwatosa East. Jim has been caught in the middle of the conflict with the coach and with Jake. The son is now barely speaking to the father. The coach and Jim are enemies. Jim and his former wife Sandy are at odds. It is all a mess. What a bitter reminder of how things like this can spiral out of control.
>
> I obviously worry that maybe I am too into the whole thing myself. As much as I enjoy being the parent of a player, I can see in others, in Tammy, in myself how tough it is—and we make it tougher on our kids. I had hoped to learn to do this right, but so far I have not. Distancing myself is not right, but neither is Jim's obsession. Like him I lean toward going overboard. Balance is not easy, but it is what I need to find in my unbalanced life.

Then suddenly, without warning, things began to improve for Andrew—playing time increased appreciably, shots began to fall consistently, people began to notice admiringly. It was almost as if the first anniversary of his diagnosis of diabetes signaled that it was time to begin a new chapter. As Andrew's confidence rebounded, by season's end he was having the impact that was hoped for from the beginning. In assessing his junior year, I had to admit that Andrew's attitude was so much more patient and even-keeled than my own had been throughout. He never voiced a single complaint, even when he found himself on the fringes. He kept quiet and kept working hard. What I was supposed to be setting as an example for him was everything he displayed in spite of me.

The respect he had earned from opposing coaches brought post-season honors, but, even better, his teammates voted him winner of the Christian Leadership award. As he announced Andrew to be the recipient, Milwaukee Lutheran's coach described this as the award that best exemplified the team's motto of "Honoring God, Honoring Team, and Honoring Self," in that order. So, was his junior year a success? "The cup is more than half full," I reflected after the team banquet. "In fact, it overflows." While I wasted too much of my time agonizing, Andrew was certainly not wasting his.

The tide of momentum had shifted, and he would ride the wave into the summer before his senior year and final season at Milwaukee Lutheran. As long as he was surfing along smoothly it eased my silly suffering. Andrew had come a long way since wondering whether diabetes might prevent him from playing basketball anymore. Of course, the rather brazen dream of competing collegiately at a Division I school meant he still had so far to go. Not as far as I did, I realized.

Nearly three decades had passed since I had last played in high school and first played in college, and now I had been a university president for several years, but I still had much to learn and relearn. This was not the first time in my life that I had allowed basketball to drive me nuts. Variously attributed to Benjamin Franklin, or Mark Twain, or Albert Einstein, the definition of insanity is doing the same thing over and over again and expecting it to turn out different. Perhaps that is not a clinical definition, but I kept resorting to attitudes and behaviors that had only and always failed me in the past, even though by now I knew better. Had I not already learned this lesson? I knew there was a better way.

Once in a while, when people saw me still dressed in my standard college president uniform and wearing my signature bow tie, they said it reminded them of Paul Simon, the former senator from Illinois. Indeed, there are not many members of the bow-tie-wearers club, and fewer still are famous men. The other Paul Simon, who gained fame pairing with Art Garfunkel, did not wear a bow tie, though he did have a scarf around his neck on the cover of their 1970 album, *Bridge over Troubled Water.* Andrew's "dreams were on their way," maybe "his time had come to shine," and he was figuring out how to ride that wave and "sail on by." Meanwhile, I never learned to swim well enough to avoid going under troubled waters of my own making over and again. I needed a bridge, not for the first time, and certainly not the last.

Of course, no one would ever have known that just looking at me. Nattily attired in suit and bow tie sartorial splendor, I was president of an institution of higher learning who surely spent his time pondering higher things. Principal Paul Bahr may have been suspicious, and my wife, Tammy, knew only too well, but my lunacy was mostly private, between my journal and me. I would not be convicted by a jury of my peers, but something else Paul Simon said was a description that fit me better than my peculiar neckwear:

"Still crazy after all these years, yes, still crazy after all these years."

"THE STROKE OF MIDNIGHT"
CHAPTER 5

November 1977–May 1978 —At the stroke of midnight the original Cinderella story takes an unhappy twist. The dream-come-true scenario, after a brief but spectacular attention-grabbing moment, unravels once the bell tolls twelve o'clock. Grim gradually gives way to something grand by the end of the fairy tale, however, and everyone lives happily ever after. That is what makes the fable so fabulous. "Cinderella" teams in college basketball, by contrast, are rags to riches real-life sensations that charm us for awhile but seldom have celebratory conclusions. Sure, surprise teams unexpectedly make an incredible run, punch their ticket to the "Big Dance," and get everybody excited. Nevertheless, at some point midnight strikes, dreams are dashed, and the story recedes from the headlines.

The St. John's College "Ferry Tale" never approached becoming a Cinderella story. Our poor team was too wrapped in rags ever to get a sniff of riches. The "Johnnie Spirit," as the college's regular old school bus was euphemistically dubbed, was painted burnt orange. This was our carriage to every road game, but it was not designed for traveling in style. In fact, it rather looked like a pumpkin on wheels. A couple of weeks had passed since Halloween jack-o-lanterns welcomed trick-or-treaters on front porches around Winfield. It only felt like early September, but instead it was a mid-November Monday afternoon when we finished our lunch in the Campus Center, grabbed our orange away-game uniforms, and climbed on board the bus.

The "Johnnie Spirit" idled a few minutes in the parking lot directly across the street from the gymnasium. The boys' team got on first and crowded together in the back followed by the players on the girls' team, who squeezed two per seat in the front section. Our pre-game meals of peanut butter and jelly or bologna and cheese sandwiches, carrot sticks, and apples were distributed around for later. Once everybody was settled, Ralph Skov—sometimes English professor, sometimes basketball coach, and sometimes bus driver—stepped on the gas pedal and steered the "Johnnie Spirit" straight for the state line. We were heading out of Winfield en route to our first game of the season in Tonkawa, just over the Oklahoma border, with little hype and huge hope. Hints of optimism always accompany the opener, when the loss column of the team's record is still unblemished. Regrettably, our season, like the compass on our school bus, immediately headed south.

Cracking the starting lineup was my main objective once practice got underway. This was the same goal I'd had in mind before I set foot on campus. In order to transfer to a bigger, better program in the next year or two, I assumed a starting position was a minimum credential. Chris Peterson had higher aspirations for me, "I'm still expecting you to become all-world," he exaggerated, "Play the way Pat Ferry can play and everything will work out." All-world, whatever that might be, was probably outside my orbit, and even finding my name listed on the starting five would be a reach. How would I measure up?

The competition to start at guard promised to be fierce. I was completely intimidated by the two black kids from Ohio: Vince Johnson, a lanky 6'7" guy who played post, and Scott Wallace from Lutheran High School East in Cleveland, who, unfortunately, was a guard like me. At Jefferson we played in a lily-white suburban conference, and the only black kid we faced during my senior year was now on a full-ride scholarship to the University of Hawaii. The rosters of teams from the inner-city's Denver Prep League, in contrast to our Jefferson County League, always had several black athletes, and among them were perennially some of the best players in the state. Now I would have to compete with inner-city black kids for playing time, and I did not like my chances.

Vince and Scott moved into the room next door and instantly cranked up the volume on the Commodores'"Brick House" much louder than I dared play music on my own stereo. My assumption was that they were also going to be making more noise on the team than I. Their swagger elevated my concerns. Both of them were downright mouthy, but I supposed that they could probably back up all the trash talk on the court before I ever saw them play. Neither my prejudices nor my prejudgments were too far off. Once practice officially started it was clear that Vince and Scott were shoo-ins to be among the first five.

I likewise figured Ralph would start his son, Erik, who was also a first-year freshman. Erik Skov was much better at guitar than he was at basketball. He was a big fan of the southern band Lynyrd Skynyrd. In their famous hit "Sweet Home Alabama" the band took jabs at rock star Neil Young ("I hope Neil Young will remember, a southern man don't need him around anyhow.") Erik was more eclectic. He liked Neil Young, too. He strummed his guitar, accompanied himself on the harmonica, and sang a screechy falsetto—Erik was a "Neil Young wannabe." But, he did not especially want to be a basketball player. Playing on the team was little more than a diversion, but Erik was sure to see plenty of action "since he had the same address as the coach," I wrote to my own parents. He went out of his way to befriend me, and while I appreciated the gesture the thought of playing behind him was aggravating to me.

Conceding a guard spot to Scott Wallace was tough enough, but losing a starting job to Erik Skov was harder to swallow. "It doesn't appear that I'll start even though I should," I complained to Billie and Lefty, "Coach Skov has his son ahead of me." Scott Wallace was from inner-city Cleveland and must have had some high-caliber game, but what truly rankled me was that "Erik didn't even make first-team at Winfield High." The whole situation smacked of rank nepotism and, I admitted, "It is not much fun being ripped off." I let my parents know that rumors around campus had me in a reserve role relegated to coming off the bench.

Billie promptly replied:

I wouldn't worry about rumors. You've always had to prove yourself, haven't you? When I was cleaning out your stuff I ran across a letter from Rick Peterson when he was starting at St. John's. He was concerned about whether or not he would be starting and/or making the traveling squad. He always had to prove his ability, too .... I hope basketball goes well for you. I'm sure it will—just

pretend you're back at Jefferson and play like you did then. You'll
be great!

Neither pretending that I was still at Jefferson, nor wishing on a
star, nor wishing I was a star would make much difference. I just had
to prove myself in practice. Mom supposed a little make-believe might
be helpful for inspiring my own performance. It was becoming abundantly clear that the Eagle team had issues that transcended who finally
were given starting nods whether by virtue of talent or of birthright.
Practice alone would not be enough. We desperately needed someone
somewhere to wave a wand and miraculously make the entire team
better. Billie Ferry, was my mother but she was not a fairy godmother.
There was nothing she could offer except encouragement. Soon after
official practice sessions convened I warned her that we were "looking
very bad." Nevertheless, personally I was hungry to have enough of an
impact to draw some attention higher up the college basketball food
chain. If I just was given the chance.

I held my own, even with Scott Wallace, in practice. Each day, my
confidence grew as my sense for where I stacked up competitively
was positively reinforced. The argument that I should see plenty of
minutes was bolstered by Rick Peterson, who, after watching us work
out, gave me a pep talk. I told Billie and Lefty that Rick urged me "to
shoot every time I got the ball because I'm the only one who can make
a shot." The vote of confidence was appreciated. Gaining an advantage
by outperforming some of the guys on my own team was one thing,
but faring well against more talented opposition from the tough junior
colleges programs on our schedule was another matter. "When we play
Monday night I hope I do well," I wrote, "I'm sure going to try hard."

All of my college basketball fantasies were about to meet up with the stiff test of hardcore, hardwood reality.

Before we left Winfield for Northern Oklahoma College, any worries about sitting on the bench had vanished. My own performance in practice was less a factor than the announcement a few days ahead of the opener that Vince and Scott had been suspended for a couple of games. Ralph didn't tell us why, but the word in the dormitory was that they were accused of shoplifting. "Actually, we're better off without them," I insisted in a letter, "When they play they shoot every time they touch the ball. We really lack any idea of what it means to play as a team."

Coach Skov called me into his office and told me to become the team leader and quarterback. "I'd really like to," I continued, "but it will be difficult considering I'll get no cooperation from the black guys when they come back." Billie beamed at the coach's compliment. She also had a little advice: "You are very intelligent and diplomatic. Why can't you reach the dissenters, or trouble makers, or bad boys and make them realize they hurt the team?" Perhaps she understood my real problem, "If they know they can intimidate all of you they will." Though far away, Billie still had a knack for reading what was going on in my mind. At least for the Northern Oklahoma game, cooperation from Vince and Scott was inconsequential. They watched in street clothes from the stands. My mother wished she could join them. "How I would love to be there! Take care, play well, and write us the results. If there are any write-ups in the Winfield paper be sure and send them!" She hoped maybe I would get my name in the paper.

All the guys sat in the bleachers and watched as our girls' team was pulverized by the highly touted Northern Oklahoma College women.

As the second half of the women's game got under way, we hopped down from the seats and sauntered slowly, trying to look relaxed and not nervous, toward the visitor's locker room. We dressed quickly and gathered at the chalk board to watch Ralph diagram X's and O's. Finally, it was our turn to take the floor.

Ralph was decked out in his black leisure suit with orange shirt, orange socks, and white buck shoes. His broken black horn-rimmed glasses were held together by a piece of white athletic tape at the bridge of his nose. A direct hit to the face from a basketball errantly tossed across the court by a member of the opponent's band busted his spectacles. Now Ralph was sort of a spectacle himself.

If dressing for success was the objective, then we got exactly what we deserved. The headline of the next day's *Winfield Daily Courier* requested by my mother read, "Northern Okla. Jolts SJC" and went on to describe the "112–75 rout of the St. John's Eagles." I couldn't wait for a copy of the article to write my own longer assessment of my first collegiate game:

> Well my first college game is over, and it ended on a sour note. We lost 112–75. They weren't that great but they were pretty tall. They just kept throwing it over our heads and slamming it through.

> I played pretty good, as Chris probably told you. I called him after the game. I was team captain. I don't know if I am permanently captain or not, but that doesn't really matter. I played 37 of 40 minutes. It is hard to say if I'll play that much every game. I scored 20 points but should have had at least 10 more. I also had 6 assists but should have had at least 12, which is the school record. I would have had 12 but guys blew easy shots. I think this is the first time I have

averaged 20 points even if it is only one game! I probably won't be able to keep it up as soon as the black guys get back because I won't get to shoot as much, but if I hit a good percentage who knows? Anyway it was a good start.

If this were soccer season I'd get my picture in the Winfield paper for the game. I doubt I'll get anything because Coach Skov probably won't get the report in on time. If he didn't they may not put anything in after tomorrow's paper since it will be old news. Rick Peterson said Skov is pretty bad about publicity and that the paper was pretty much at his disposal, but he never takes advantage. We didn't even get a preview article before the season while Southwestern College gets something almost every day. The reason is that Coach Skov doesn't bother putting the news in, especially for away games like yesterday. It is not that important to me, but I do wish he'd take advantage of the publicity. It's really more important for us as a junior college if players want to transfer.

It was a pretty fun trip. It only took an hour and a half which will be our second shortest trip all season. Our girls played before us and lost 108–22. They are terrible and they played the #19 team in the nation. We all stopped at McDonald's after the game and were given $2 for food. I wasn't hungry so I made some cash. It looks like road games will be my best source of income! This week we go to a tournament in Iola which is a longer drive. Since we're playing both Friday and Saturday we're staying overnight in a Best Western Motel. As long as I play well, b-ball makes things pretty fun around here

Before mailing the letter the next day I hunted down the paper and cut out several copies of the afternoon *Courier* article, without my picture but with the mention that I led the team in scoring with 20 points. Each copy was neatly folded in half and carefully tucked into the envelope with instructions written at the bottom of the letter: "P.S. Put at least one of these away somewhere for future references."

True, we lost the game in a landslide. But, all those points and all those minutes, team captain and the coach's quarterback, meal money and motels—basketball was the reason that I was in Kansas—or Oklahoma, and basketball was off to a decent if not fabulous start. Coach Skov pulled the "Johnnie Spirit" back into its designated space in the parking lot, and we stretched our legs as we got off the bus and began walking toward our rooms in Rehwinkel. I looked at the Timex Billie had given me. I should have guessed; it was almost midnight.

We would have another shot at Northern Oklahoma just before Christmas break. By then, unhappily, things had already gone from bad to worse for the team. My own production also trailed off. When we played host to them in December our losing streak was at nine and counting. With the exception of one game (in which only a four-point margin separated us from victory), every contest was no contest—one lopsided loss after another. The *Winfield Daily Courier* was challenged to find different ways to report gloomy results that soon began to sound like a broken record. Indeed, our opponents were probably breaking some records of their own along the way.

> "Cowley Point Machine Erupts for 131–68 Rout of Johnnies"—The busiest person in the St. John's Gym last night was the scorekeeper and the most pleased people were the Cowley County Tigers.

> "Barton Strikes Early Sinks Johnnies 97–72"—Barton County built

up a 24-point lead in the first half last night at the St. John's Gym and then matched points with the Johnnies the rest of the way to take a 97–72 decision over the home team.

And, in an era obviously not yet concerned about politically correct sensitivity:

"Haskell Pastes Johnnies"—Haskell's Indians held a hardwood massacre Saturday night as they scalped the St. John's College Eagles 119–75 in a non-conference basketball game.

Even a small-town paper had no nice way to tell locals the truth—the St. John's College basketball team was awful.

Following the Haskell game my level of discouragement descended to previously uncharted depths, and the outlook for the future offered few prospects for improvement. "We played last night and lost 119 to seventy-something," I wrote and then began to look ahead. "Remember that Allen County team that beat us 126–51? We play a team Tuesday (Butler County) that beat them 105–83 yesterday! The other two games scheduled this week offer no better opportunity to win. We are 0–7 and it appears we will be 0–10 for sure." Finally, frustration boiled over, and I spilled my guts in a letter to Billie and Lefty:

Needless to say I'm very disappointed—not only about basketball but the whole situation here. I'm not playing very well but our team is terrible. It is half because the coach is clueless and half because of the apathetic attitudes of everybody (except for me) on this team. I guess I should leave a little room for lack of talent of most of our guys since we're generally outclassed in most of our games. The guys on our team play solely for themselves and the coach lets them get away with everything. I can't remember getting a basket because somebody threw me a good pass. Every point I get is because of my own effort. Nobody else on the team can say that because I pass all the time.

Looking on the brighter side of it (tongue-in-cheek), Winfield has got to be the most boring place in the world. There is nothing to do here but play basketball, and, as you can see, I'm not able to benefit much from all the practice. People at this school are just not my kind of people. Nobody ever does anything worthwhile or enjoyable. My classes are tedious and I can't wait for finals to get it all over and be done.

I really don't know what to do about it all. I'm not exaggerating any of it at all. In fact, if anything it is worse than I describe it—particularly the basketball and boredom. I can't say that I think it's a good idea for me to come back next semester, all things considered. I'd have the advantage of playing nine more games, but while playing those games would give me more experience I'd also have to tolerate a lot of losing. There is no way we will turn it around …. .

I know you're bound to have a lot of questions, ideas and views, and I want some advice. I know you, Mom, are usually pretty opinionated about things like this and would prefer me to 'stick it out' despite the consequences. I only ask that you look at both options from all angles.

"Northern Tops SJC Again"—Any hopes the St. John's College Eagles had of avenging their earlier loss to Northern Oklahoma faded quickly at the Eagles' Nest Saturday night when the visitors struck early and went on to pound the Johnnies 84–49."

Our record fell to 0–10, and it was the end of the first semester. My dreams had turned to nightmares, and the only happy ending I could envision was escaping Winfield once and for all.

It seemed less a question of *whether* than a matter of *when* I would throw in the towel. Before I finished final exams and prepared to travel home, however, I was still considering my options about whether to return after Christmas:

> At least by coming back I can give the season a chance to come around. If I'm still unhappy I won't finish. I really want to play big college and I doubt another month of experience could hurt me. The only question I have is can I stand this team, this school, this town for even one more month? I'm not sure.

> I really love playing basketball and the thought of quitting, even if it is only temporarily, is kind of sickening. I'm not really sure what we have here is what should be called basketball, at least not basketball as I know it.

> My biggest goal is to play ball next year at a big school in a class organization. I have to take the steps necessary to reach that goal, and I don't know whether staying would be helpful or a hindrance.

> I'm really confused right now. I don't like being unhappy, but there is so much to think about. I'm not going to stick it out merely to stick it out. I don't need my character built much further. My decisions will have to be made with my best interests, both present and far-reaching, in mind.

Parenting had no doubt become an onerous task for Billie, and I was her labor-intensive, faraway child. Each day I looked forward to getting letters from family and friends, but Billie must have had mixed feelings opening her box to discover an envelope with another missive from me. She had to temper her impulse simply to prescribe what, in her opinion, I ought to do. Yet, it was obvious that I coveted her advice. Sustaining an argument through the mail is more difficult than face-to-face encounters. Instead of arguing, Billie carefully balanced concern and counsel. The matter was weighty enough that Lefty also weighed in. In the end the decision was up to me. At some point a boy had to become a man. Mom wrote:

> Hi! We received your letter yesterday and feel badly that you were so down. There is no reason for you to feel that way. I mean we only want you to do what is best for you in every way. If you can't stand the place, people, etc. you don't have to stay there. Nothing is worth being miserable over. Dad said if you stick it out 'fine and dandy' if you don't 'fine and dandy.' It is what you want not anyone else. And what we want is for you to be happy with what you're doing—not happy as in having fun all the time, but contented and pleased with your progress.
>
> A few letters ago you said attitude was the big thing in a winning team. I know you've tried, but when the others don't have it or aren't team players, I don't know what more you can do. You've always been almost too unselfish when playing and that's something you can't change and wouldn't want to. I know you will be able to walk on and make it. It isn't always handed to you—you will make it and if you can't do it there you will do it someplace else ... .
>
> And if Chris gets a good deal it will be because he has dedicated himself entirely to it. That's not putting you down so don't get

upset with me over that. He plays constantly—it is his entire life and nothing interferes with it. I would rather you have a more rounded life than that and I know you enjoy doing other things now and then.

Anyway, Pat, we're behind you whatever you decide. Just make sure when you do decide that you have no regrets. If you should go back you would really be miserable after basketball is over (even more than now) since you don't like the town, etc. If you don't go back you might be just as miserable here if you aren't playing win or lose. It is really a tough thing for you, but as you know life is full of these decisions and you grow with each one of them. Take care and don't worry. What will be will be.

Over Christmas break I decided that nine games in January before the start of second semester was enough to entice me to return to campus at least for a few weeks. My mind, however, was made up. By the end of the month I would leave St. John's College and go home. The Jan-term period was three weeks in duration, and we were required to take one course. A Spanish class at Southwestern College was the perfect solution. I enrolled but never once attended. Skipping classes on our small campus would have been too conspicuous, but this way nobody bothered to check up on me. My calendar was clear except for practices and games. Letters and late nights—January was a good opportunity to catch up on my correspondence and sleep in the next morning.

Not long after I got back to Winfield myself, three carloads from Colorado converged on Kansas. Bill and Ardith Peterson, my brothers Bob and Bill, and a couple of high school buddies still on break from college each made the trip to St. John's and were in the crowd for our weekend tournament in early January. Somebody from back home was finally attending one of my college games, and I was thrilled to be taking the floor with them in town to watch me play. I had almost forgotten what it felt like to get psyched-up for a game.

The tournament's format was a round-robin. We played three other Lutheran colleges (I was told they were affiliated with St. John's) beginning on Thursday night with Concordia College from Austin, Texas. The 69 points that we scored in the second half was impressive but still not enough. The final score found us on the losing end of 99–86. For the first time since the opener I scored 20 points. Scott Wallace led us with 27 and Vince Johnson added 14. I was content that our team showed a few flashes of competence and did not embarrass ourselves in front of my family and friends.

On Friday we were paired against St. Paul's College from Concordia, Missouri. St. Paul's had lost the night before 108-49, so at last we found a team that might be as woeful as we were. Hoping for a continuation of the momentum of the second half scoring barrage from our previous game, we found ourselves in an unusual situation as players were being introduced. We looked each other in the eye with a gleam that came with recognition that we had a legitimate chance to win. By the halftime intermission we had a 45–38 advantage and were wild-eyed with excitement. Storming into the locker room with shouts and cheers, we slapped each other on the back and could not wait to go back out and finish the job. The victory celebration, however, was a bit premature. According to the *Courier*, "Things went downhill in the second half with St. Paul's finally struggling into the lead." Now fear shown in our eyes as once again we seemed destined to find a way to lose.

Not on this night, not in this close of a contest, not in front of fans who had traveled that far to see me—not to be denied! "Pat Ferry didn't score many points for the St. John's College Eagles last night, but he came up with two at just the right time as the Johnnies nipped St. Paul's of Concordia, Missouri 67–66 for their first win of the campaign after 11 losses." I may have "netted only six tallies for the game," the *Courier* continued, but the Johnnies snatched victory from the jaws of defeat on my last-second shot. Judging from our spontaneous exuberance as the final buzzer sounded, you would have thought we had won the NCAA Championship.

Our postgame party downtown on Main Street at Joe's City Cigar Store, the local pub popular with college students, did not have a salutary effect on our third and final game of the weekend Saturday night. Concordia College from Milwaukee, Wisconsin, halted our season's longest winning streak at one. We were back on track. Too bad it was a track heading the wrong direction. My farewells to the folks who had made the long trip to see me play included the comment that I would likely see them all again in a few weeks. Our team's sudden improved play did not divert me from my plan. The unexpected news that followed during the middle of the next week made it appear as if there was really no other choice.

When we arrived at the gymnasium the following week for our next game against Central College, Coach Skov announced that Vince Johnson and Scott Wallace were academically ineligible for the rest of the season. This bolt out of the blue, it struck me, had to be fatal. There was no way we could recover. Although we played without the Ohioans for the first two or three games of the year, by early January the circumstances had completely changed. Placing this news alongside injuries and defections from players who had already abandoned the team, and suddenly only four players remained on the roster for the Central game.

Of the four of us left Tim Pollum was the only sophomore. He was from Bonner Springs in suburban Kansas City who had come to campus with plans to teach and coach grade school children in a Lutheran school. He was looking for a position at a place like Bethlehem Lutheran, I imagined, where the Peterson boys attended. Pollum was ostensibly the one among us with a full year of collegiate experience behind him, but that was a little misleading. He was nicknamed "Two-point Timmy" in honor of the entirety of his scoring output during his freshman year.

Paul Birner was a 6'3" freshman from Greenbelt, Maryland who was mainly a soccer player. His primary reason for enrolling at St. John's was to become a Lutheran pastor. Wry sense of humor and sarcastic wit were, in my opinion, his most significant contributions to the team. Once Ralph neglected to fill the tank of the "Johnnie Spirit" after a road trip and we ran out of gas only blocks from campus. The boys unloaded and pushed the bus the quarter mile toward the nearest filling station. Just as we finally reached the other more favorable side of a hill that could have propelled us forward one of Winfield's finest raced up with siren screaming and "pulled us over." He guessed mischief, but once Ralph explained our plight the cop asked if we intended to go to the one station on that side of town, which by now was only a stone's throw away. Paul instantly replied, "We thought we might shop around first and choose based on where we could get the best price." Later, after we finally reached our destination and just before the game, Paul needed to use the restroom. On his way back out he walked toward the door to exit when one of the Hesston College fans chided him saying, "At

Hesston College we are taught to wash our hands after we use the urinal." Paul quickly retorted, "At St. John's College they teach us not to pee on our hands." Now our team's starting post player, Paul Birner helped us rebound from our dismal difficulties with a little levity better than he collected caroms off the glass.

The other two holdovers were Erik Skov, who now unquestionably deserved to be a starter, and me. By itself this was no fearsome foursome. But, whether we were a daunting quartet or not made no difference since at least a quintet, regardless of its skill level, was required to play. Forfeit was a realistic alternative, but Central had already departed on the two-hour drive from McPherson. Ralph was sure they would want at least to scrimmage rather than waste the whole trip. A phone call was made to Rehwinkel Hall dormitory for reinforcements.

Fortunately, somebody answered and didn't just let it ring. Four guys who had never played college basketball before—I doubted any of them had ever played in high school—rushed to the gym and put on uniforms. "Central Clubs Johnnies 91–56," the paper said the next day. Given the situation, the clubbing could have been much worse.

If our beleaguered boys were out of their league before the mid-season purge, the makeshift squad frantically assembled to finish out was not even a match for most college intramural teams. Four more walk-ons joined the squad, giving us twelve warm bodies but very few basketball players. My apprehensions about making the starting unit in October would have been welcome worries in mid-January. At least at the beginning we had something faintly resembling a basketball team. Not so any more.

The nadir was reached at Barton County Community College in Great Bend. Although the paper said, "Pat Ferry, 6'1" freshman guard, was a bright spot for St. John's scoring 19 points," the simple headline covered the sad saga with all the news anybody needed to know, "St. John's loses 142–44." We were defeated by an almost incomprehensible margin of 98 points. For the last minute of the game and for the first time all season we intentionally slowed it down to kill the clock. I dribbled away from defenders, waiting for time to expire in attempts to avert being defeated by 100. Two nights later at Coffeyville I scored 13 points to lead the team, but we fell 120–31. Coach Skov's post-game comment quoted in the *Winfield Daily Courier* would have been laughable if it were not so painful. 'They're very tough and they hit exceptionally well,' he said about Coffeyville, 'But, it was a very clean game. There were only 12 fouls. I thought both teams played very well.'

Suddenly our situation had become almost surreal—stalling late in the game to keep our atrocious defeat under triple digits and avoiding foul trouble in the next outing as our only measures of success. "Enough," I cried, "Uncle!" Actually, I called my brother, Bob, who braved icy roads all the way to make another trip to Winfield to come and deliver me home.

All my belongings, including the stereo, records, and Raleigh, fit more easily into the back of his Volvo station wagon than they had in the trunk of the Granada. I grabbed the bedspread off my bunk and the Converse canvas high tops out of the closet, shook hands with Reed and Erik, and said good-bye. My brother retraced the route Lefty drove not so many months before. The furnace blast of summer was replaced by the blustery chill of winter. The radio played softly in the background, but it did not interrupt our 550-mile conversation. Not once did I doze or drift off. We talked about Billie and Lefty and the rest of our family. We talked about college and basketball. My brother was more than willing to explore the obvious question provoked by my departure from Kansas, "What's next?"

I didn't have the courage to tell him, but I already had a hunch that I knew the answer to that question. Before we made it home to Denver, before we reached Salina or even Wichita, before we crossed the Walnut River and watched Winfield disappear in the rear view mirror, I more or less knew. Before my brother ever even showed up in Kansas to transport me to Colorado, his nerves jangled from navigating snow and ice, I believed that I knew. In fact, the moment I hung up the phone after an atypical collect call home asking somebody to come and get me, I was fairly certain that I knew the answer to the question, "What's next?" Finally, after five months, I was ready, and in my soul I knew it already.

Still, I went home with him anyway. After all, Bob had gone to such trouble. I stayed home long enough to watch my old Jefferson teammates win a game en route to the state tournament, where they would come within a hair's breadth of winning the state championship. Chris Peterson would go on to lead Colorado preps in scoring and eventually sign a national letter-of-intent to attend Creighton University in the Missouri Valley Conference. The Saints were on the march. Before the season started, Billie had urged me "to pretend that I was back at Jefferson," in hopes that I would play with more confidence. Now that I was back at Jefferson I was not playing basketball at all. The team that I watched win that night was not mine. My team was in Winfield losing our rematch with Cowley County 130–31. That was where I belonged. As soon as my brother left a few days later to return to his home in Minneapolis, I quickly packed a suitcase with only my bare essentials and told Billie and Lefty that I was taking a bus back to Kansas. Kansas?

Why Kansas? Neither of them asked. I was grateful they didn't because I was unsure I could explain. I just knew. They seemed satisfied that I was convinced it was the right thing to do.

Upon my return to campus I sent my parents a post card: "Dear Mom and Dad, I need $785 from my account for this semester. Everybody was surprised and pleased to see me back, and I am glad I am here. We play Pratt tonight." I only missed two games during my brief hiatus. Coach Skov and the team received me with open arms. The boys from Pratt offered only a rude welcome:

> When Pratt's Al Taylor broke loose for an unmolested slam-dunk before the game was five seconds old it served as an omen of the bad that was to come for the St. John's Eagles on their home court last night.

"Pratt Pummels SJC 126–42," not much had changed while I was gone. Except for me—I guess I had changed a lot.

When the season finally and mercifully ended, I took the opportunity to review playing on what was arguably the worst team in the history of college basketball. Our single victory by a single point was a fluke and would not have been repeated had we faced St. Paul's College a second time. They had the unlucky misfortune of a schedule that had them face us before our two best athletes were declared ineligible for the remainder of the season. From that point on there was never a question about whether we would win or lose our next game. Ralph could not inspire us with the old line that our opponents put on their Chuck Taylor Converses one foot at a time as evidence that they were merely human, just like us. Besides, it was impossible to take our coach seriously in his black leisure suit, orange shirt, orange socks, and white buck shoes even after he got a new pair of black horn-rimmed glasses. Every time we took the floor on our home court, or every time we boarded the "Johnnie Spirit" to travel to a road game, we knew the outcome of the contest in advance. None of us were prescient or prophetic. We were losers, plain and simple. Pratt dunked on us within the first five seconds, but every game, even before the ball was ever tipped, we knew we were going to be slaughtered.

The St. John's yearbook's summary of our season sought to put it as softly as possible:

> Despite a disappointing season, scores don't always tell the whole story. At the end of each game played the Eagles may have seemed to be on the short end of things, but mental victories were scored. Amid team member losses and unseasoned replacements, the Eagles showed spirit, togetherness, and personal victory. The Eagles should be commended for working together as a team, boosting spirits and never giving up. Twelve players received letters and Pat Ferry was selected captain for next year's team.

Which mental or personal victories each of us scored were not exactly clear. While the scores may not have told the whole story, it was a stretch to say that the Eagles only "seemed to be on the short end of things" at the end of each game played. We were definitely on the short end. As ample documentation of that fact, and as a record of my freshman-year futility for posterity, the yearbook included the list of our scores throughout the season. The kind words of the editor's summary were in marked contrast to the results printed alongside:

Scores

SJC		Opp
75	Northern Oklahoma	112
51	Allen County	126
57	Seward County	84
68	Cowley County	131
72	Barton County	97
75	Haskell	119
75	Highland	79
53	Butler County	66
57	Pratt	101
49	Northern Oklahoma	84
86	Concordia Austin	99
67	St. Paul's	66
60	Concordia Milwaukee	82
56	Central	91
48	Hesston	102
44	Barton County	142
31	Cowley County	130
44	Cloud County	100
42	Pratt	126
37	Haskell	96
56	Central	76
39	Cloud County	111
58	Hesston	81
47	York	109

Far from becoming a dream come true, my personal "Ferry Tale" was no Cinderella story. Nevertheless, I came to agree that despite a disappointing season "scores don't always tell the whole story." Struggling through months of homesickness, depression, and aggravation nearly drove me from St. John's many times before my brother actually did drive me away. The arrival of spring brought a transformation. Winfield's trees blossomed, flowers bloomed, and gradually I came out of my shell. I even went to a dance on campus upstairs in Academy Hall. Near the end of the evening I worked up the courage to ask one of the high school girls who crashed the college sock-hop with a couple of friends to dance. After the slow song ended and we stepped apart I took the even bolder step to ask her out on a date even though I had never met her before that night. Turns out that her name was Tammy, and she was the daughter of my psychology teacher, Professor Saleska. I borrowed Reed's orange Volkswagen beetle, which looked more like a pumpkin than the "Johnnie Spirit," and we drove to Wichita for a movie and then out for pizza. Thankfully, she had stuck a dollar in her pocket before we left her house because I didn't have quite enough to pay the bill. Not a late date and a dollar short—I hurried to have her home before midnight.

"Talk about Beginner's Luck!" the card I sent to Billie in May for Mother's Day read, "The First Time Around and I Got You for a Mother!" On the inside of the card I wrote, "This will probably be the last mail that you get from me from Kansas this year." Actually, my letter-writing had tapered off slightly second semester—enough, however, so that Billie chided me a few times for faltering and dereliction of duty. Those were not charges that could be leveled at her. In appreciation I wrote:

Thanks for doing all the many wonderful things you have done all year. You were very understanding and helpful my first year away, even if you weren't too nearby. I promise it will be smoother sailing from now on.

Nevertheless, don't ever think your kindness goes unnoticed. It doesn't. I praise and thank God for such a wonderful family and especially for you, Mom. I love you and miss you. Take care.

Love, Pat

I had come a long way, much farther than the 550 miles Lefty and Billie drove to bring me from Denver to Winfield and my brother Bob drove to return me from Kansas to Colorado. The direction I took, however, was unanticipated. Chris Peterson's prediction that I would become "all-world" did not quite pan out. However, the same year, a rock star whose name was out of this world had a smash hit that shook the planet. *Stomp, stomp, clap … stomp, stomp, clap … stomp, stomp, clap*—Freddie Mercury, lead vocalist of the British band, Queen, sang the song, officially called "News of the World," that was being played over the loud speakers at nearly every gym in which we played. The crowd accompanied him, "We will, we will rock you … *stomp, stomp, clap … stomp, stomp, clap* … We will, we will rock you … *stomp, stomp, clap.*" Then the fans would clap and clap as their boys proceeded to stomp us. The album's title cut was then immediately followed by Mercury's less confrontational but no less confident and no less famous song, "We are the Champions":

I've paid my dues, time after time.

I've done my sentence but committed no crime.

And bad mistakes, I've made a few.

I've had my share of sand kicked in my face,

but I've come through.

We are the champions, my friends,

and we'll keep on fighting till the end.

We are the champions,

we are the champions,

no time for losers

'cause we are the champions of the world.

Dues paid, sentence served, bad mistakes, sand kicked in our face—I could relate to all of that stuff and in spades. News of our world drew scant attention, even in the *Winfield Daily Courier*. Nobody voted for me for first-team all-world, or even first-team all-conference. I barely made first-team on arguably the worst team ever. The St. John's College Eagles never rocked anybody's world much less won title "champions of the world." We were most definitely not the champions of the world. Somewhere along the way during my freshman year, however, my whole world changed when I found out about what it meant to be "more than conquerors."

"SHOTS IN THE DARK"
CHAPTER 6

May 2007–May 2008 —"A shot in the dark"—sometimes the only way to find out is to give it a try. Admittedly, when odds are long and chances for success are slim, a big fat zero is usually the outcome. Is it worth the energy and effort when, safe to say, the vast majority of shots in the dark unceremoniously miss their mark? Risk is typically commensurate with reward, however, and the longer the shot the bigger the potential pay-off. Nothing ventured, nothing gained. Besides, you never know when you might get lucky. Almost two centuries before my high school was named in his honor, Thomas Jefferson offered his own insight into luck. Jefferson said, "I am a great believer in luck and I find the harder I work, the more I have of it." Work hard and then give it a shot.

In early 2004 we extended an invitation to one of Jefferson's successors, President George W. Bush, to be the commencement speaker for our May graduation at Concordia. The commander-in-chief normally speaks to graduating classes of one of the military academies each year, and occasionally he delivers a speech at commencement exercises elsewhere. Our connections to the White House were tenuous at best, but we worked them for all they were worth and then sent a letter to 1600 Pennsylvania Avenue.

On April 1, 2004, the honorable recipient of our invitation defied expectations and agreed to come. The subsequent public announcement followed later the same day. Most on campus assumed the release of information was a poor attempt at an April Fools' Day joke. Depending on one's political persuasion Mr. Bush's presence on our campus was not consistently viewed as positive for the university. Critics said we were the fools, and the compilation of hate mail that I assembled as part of the memorabilia from the event resulted in a hefty tome. It was a long shot, and not everyone supported me, but I certainly felt lucky to have the sitting President of the United States of America come to Concordia.

A few years later I took another shot at a world-famous graduation speaker, or more accurately I made a pitch to "Home Run King" Henry Aaron to come to Concordia. As a boy being raised in Denver before expansion brought the Colorado Rockies to town, I was bereft of a local team or big-league ballplayers to support. My buddies and I established whatever criteria made most sense to us and selected our own heroes and baseball clubs to cheer accordingly. My favorite was Hank Aaron, and I was a fan of the Atlanta Braves until he left to finish his career in Milwaukee. Personal affinities followed Hank, and I became a Brewers booster long before I ever set foot in Wisconsin. He was still revered in Milwaukee, but I never had the occasion to meet Hank Aaron.

One of Concordia's nearby neighbors, Joe Kennedy, was introduced to me by a mutual acquaintance. By happy happenstance I learned Joe was Hank Aaron's oldest and dearest friend, dating back to their years growing up in Mobile, Alabama. With Mr. Kennedy as intermediary, I invited his boyhood buddy and my boyhood idol to Concordia. Hank's prior experience speaking for college graduations was limited to only a single other occasion. Previously he had addressed the graduates of Harvard University. Concordia was in select company, therefore, when Mr. Aaron accepted our invitation. Nobody enjoyed his company that day more than I. It was a long shot, and I felt lucky to have one of the world's truly all-time great athletes and my personal all-time favorite ballplayer present on our campus.

Sports reporters converged on Concordia to ask Henry Aaron questions at the press conference arranged before commencement, but there were also a few questions aimed my way. Word had begun to leak that the St. Louis Rams football team was considering our campus for the site of their summer training camp. Concordia and several other colleges in Wisconsin and Illinois were visited by the Rams, who were seeking relief from the oppressive summers of St. Louis. Originally ours was not among the institutions listed on their itinerary. When we read in the paper that aides were being dispatched on a scouting mission to check out possible sites, we took a shot in the dark and made contact. At our urging they toured our lovely campus, with its incomparably beautiful Lake Michigan setting. We convinced them that it was "cooler by the lake," and after their visit we thought it was cool that they chose Concordia. We were lucky to have the bonanza of publicity that accompanied hosting a National Football League franchise that used our facilities for three weeks.

Of course, most of my shots in the dark have never seen the light of day, much less made the newspapers or television. Scores of long shots

I have attempted have fallen way short, and often I have failed to score. For every time I have followed Thomas Jefferson's advice and worked hard enough to manage to get a little lucky, there have been countless other hard luck examples of hard work unrewarded. Still, there is little room for pouting since I have experienced more than my fair share of positive results. Has it been mere coincidence that much of my "luck" the past decade has been associated with my position, some of it hard work but some of it hardly working, as Concordia's president? I am not so naïve as to suppose that rank is without privileges.

Even writing this story and imagining that it might be read was a shot in the dark. My chances of success were dramatically improved, however, because of my office. An unknown president of an obscure small college does not approach celebrity status. Nevertheless, with my connections to lots of people in all kinds of places, the audience of potential readers was increased exponentially. Maybe my memoir was intrinsically interesting and written with enough panache to deserve attention regardless. Or maybe not. This much was undeniable; I would never have bothered to tell the tale except for the fact that I was familiar with angles to get attention. Being a college president offers unusually extensive, though not unlimited, entrée. The extent to which my clout carried in the case of this book, for instance, would be tested by whether this sentence was ever read outside the intimate inner circle of immediate family and close friends. Building on Jefferson's insight, it could be said that I was a great believer in luck, and I have found the more leverage that I am able to assert, the luckier I turned out to be!

How much leverage could I assert not just to get a book out but to help determine the outcome of the unfolding story before it was written? Could my lunacy be channeled into productivity? Andrew worked hard on long shots day and night. Nobody deserved success more than he did. Yet, his odds of securing a scholarship to a Division I program at the conclusion his junior season were somewhere between slim and none and leaning closer to the latter. The long-awaited growth spurt was in process, but he was still undersized. With diabetes under control and insulin injections covering the considerable consumption of his regular diet, Andrew was no longer skinnier than ever. But, he was still skinny. You just didn't see many guards with bodies like his playing at college basketball's highest level. Long odds did not deter Andrew, and he refused to let loose of his dream. He was going to need a little luck and a lot of labor to achieve his goal. How could I help him?

Parenting is an art. Assuming that we are able to overcome the impulse to live out our own dreams through the lives of our children, which was still questionable in my case, we next have to help them navigate between fantasy and reality. If we are successful they will willingly and cheerfully settle for a soft landing on the moon when their reach for the stars comes up a little short. Andrew's aims, however, were loftier than the peak of high-arching three-pointers practiced each night in the driveway. Flood lights beamed, but his were shots in the dark that aimed beyond the apex of his jumper into the night sky, and beyond the mere moon to the shining stars above. *Aspera ad astra:* Andrew might have translated the phrase in Mr. Darien's high school Latin class at Milwaukee Lutheran. Indeed, he sought to translate it into action every night in our backyard "shooting for the stars." Maybe I was a lunatic, but pushing Andrew to settle for the moon prematurely seemed almost cruel to me.

The summer AAU schedule included several high-profile tournaments and a couple of basketball camps with college recruiters in attendance. These, coupled with his senior season at Milwaukee Lutheran, would define Andrew's options without my interjecting too much too soon. Besides, you never know what will happen. Andrew, after all, could shoot the lights out! So the question left to me was clear. Could my own position be leveraged to help him be lucky enough to reach his goal of playing Division I college basketball? The only way to find out was to give it a try. If parenting was an art, maybe as a father who was also a college president I could paint a picture that would draw the attention of some college coaches. Once his junior year was over I went to work.

If a picture is worth a thousand words, then a video ought to be able to say much more. Coaches are accustomed to getting game tapes from aspiring athletes, so our strategy to ship videos in order to generate interest was not novel. Game tape was not an exception, so Andrew's had to be artfully done in order to stand out above the rest to catch somebody's eye. Incapable of tackling the task alone, I hired a staff of two to assist in the production of a highlight tape. Our youngest son, Stephen, accepted the labor-intensive duty of reviewing the digital video from every one of Andrew's games during his junior year. His job was to identify the precise moment on the tape that his brother made a big shot, preferably a three-point basket. For his many hours of painstaking persistence Stephen was paid all of $30, practically slave labor but spending money for an unemployed thirteen-year-old without an allowance. The detailed information was turned over to my nephew, James Saleska, a talented graphic design major at Concordia whose experience included assembling highlight tapes for our various teams.

Fortunately, Andrew gave us enough material to showcase his

catch-and-shoot abilities, but the quality of the video, which my nephew set to music, documented James' skills, too. The visual effect was very well done: some super slow motion here, an impressive replay there. His musical selections were subtle but helped tell the story to anyone who knew the songs or listened closely. Noize Supressor's instrumental, "Face the Future" set the tone and pointed us in the direction Andrew was looking—forward. Then, with Andrew stepping back and launching bombs on the screen, Fall Out Boy raised the question, "Am I more than you bargained for, yet?"

With shots continuing to rain down from deep, halfway through the video Flipsyde's lyrics articulated Andrew's hopes:

Some day we gonna rise up on the wind you know.

Some day we gonna dance with those lions.

Some day we gonna break free from these chains and keep on flyin'.

If you know how this is,

gonna see it's not that easy.

Don't stop get it till it's done,

from where you are or have begun.

I said keep on try a little harder to see everything you need to be.

Believe in your dreams

that you see when you're asleep.

Some day ... .

Andrew's cousin James deserved a lot of credit. All he got was a little cash. Despite the quality of the production, my hunch was not many coaches would bother to watch the tape. Even fewer would try to link lyrics to life story. If we were lucky though, a few might read a letter sent to them from a university president—even if it was a university with which they were unfamiliar and whose president was someone they did not know. The video was worth many thousands of words, but I offered a few more carefully chosen ones to make Andrew's case. The goal was simply to get him on the radar screen so that when coaches scouted AAU tournaments such as the one in late in the summer in Las Vegas, somebody might take a look.

He didn't need to impress everyone. In the end only one coach out of the dozens running the mid-major programs who received my letter and Andrew's video had to be persuaded to give him a chance. It was a long shot, but long shots, we hoped at least one Division I college coach would agree, were Andrew's forte.

The level of response exceeded my expectations. Some of the replies were perfunctory, but many were personal. Lots of letters and e-mails were written by assistants, but an equal number were from head coaches. Most promised to keep tabs on Andrew's progress over the summer. A few mentioned that their scholarships for Andrew's class were filled, but more indicated an interest in taking a closer look. Those that viewed the video affirmed my boast that Andrew was a gifted long-range shooter. The ones who were most honest also admitted that his size could pose a liability:

> Thank you for sending me the film of Andrew. I enjoyed watching him play and there is absolutely no question that he can really shoot the ball! I have been in college coaching ten years now and have rarely seen a guy who can shoot as well as Andrew does. I also agree with your assessment that the moved-back three-point line will probably not give Andrew much of a challenge.
>
> –Kieran Donohue, Assistant Coach, American University

. . . .

I finally got the tape of your son, Andrew. Coach Brenneman and I just viewed it. We both feel your son has very good upside! He is going to be a good college player. He shoots it very well and you can't ever have enough shooters on your team. We will follow him this summer.

–Kevin Broadus, Assistant Coach, Binghamton University

. . . .

Just finished watching the DVD on Andrew. As advertised he is a tremendous catch and shoot guy … . The footage certainly has me interested in evaluating him further. I will see him in Vegas … . His size may be a liability for his position, but I have seen guys his size have success at our level. After seeing him this summer we will talk again.

–Robbie Laing, Coach, Campbell University

. . . .

A father's pride for his son is an extraordinary blessing. Thank you for your wonderful letter about Andrew. I could write paragraph after paragraph about the common ground that we share, but, suffice to say, I fully understand and embrace the words that you wrote … . How will all this evolve? Always difficult to predict … .

–Bob McKillop, Head Coach, Davidson College

. . . .

At Marist we try diligently to answer every inquiry, letter of interest, etc. that we receive. Yours is certainly one of the most unique I have read in my 20 years of college coaching, given your dual position as father and college president .... Players continue to 'fall through the cracks' and go unnoticed until deep into their senior season. Keep Andrew working hard. Let's talk again next year.

–Matt Brady, Head Coach, Marist College

. . . .

I wanted to thank you for your wonderful letter and DVD regarding your son. It is rewarding, as a parent, to see other parents convey their passion for their own children. We have, at this time, no scholarships available for guards. I have kept your son's DVD for a future reference for other coaches who call me throughout the season.

–Barry Hinson, Head Coach, Missouri State University

. . . .

Thank you for your letter about your son, Andrew. He is certainly capable of playing college basketball. Your description is very accurate. The drawback is his size and strength. Our need is a 'big' shooting guard. I do wish Andrew much success.

–Phil Martelli, Head Coach, St. Joseph's University

. . . .

Andrew has a very nice shot that is pure, and he has range. We need to fill in at a lot of spots, and if we need something like him then we will shout back. We will keep him on file.

–Scott Gernander, Sam Houston State University

. . . .

I agree with your assessment of Andrew and he can shoot the ball very well. However, my honest assessment is that he is not good enough to succeed at our level. Your son does shoot it very well, and I think he can play college basketball, but he may be better at a Division II or Division III level. That is not a knock on Andrew at all. I coached at the Division III level for 8 years and know that kids at strong Division III schools are very good.

–John Becker, Director of Basketball Operations, University of Vermont

. . . .

Thank you for your letter regarding your son, Andrew. He seems like a young man who has great character and can really shoot the lights out on the court … . We are really intrigued by your son! Any time you can find someone with the ability to shoot as well as he does you are excited as a coach especially with the system that we run.

–Ben Wilkins, Assistant Coach, The College of William and Mary

Given our goal of getting a little attention, the correspondence suggested that Andrew was at least on the map. Actually, his name was all over the map thanks to an obsessive-compulsive, overzealous, lunatic-fringe father like me. When coaches from across the country converged on Las Vegas in August, it was now at least plausible that a handful would sneak a peek at one of Andrew's games. "These tournaments will be decisive in determining his chance to play at that level," I reflected, "If it all works out for him, I guess it's worth it."

"Guess" was the key word. In the weeks before the AAU trip to Las Vegas I began to second guess the entire quest. For one thing, I was a little frustrated with myself for working so hard on the project. "What has not occupied time has occupied attention. The whole thing has been fairly consuming." If Thomas Jefferson was to be trusted, all of the hard work—his on the court and mine off—should have enhanced Andrew's possibilities as a Division I college prospect. But at what price?

Andrew's summer was not an inexpensive proposition. The postage paid for the videos to be sent to all points on the compass exceeded several times over the payroll for my two-man staff. That was just the beginning. I footed the bill for a couple of trips to the East Coast where Andrew attended camps at Princeton and Columbia. The Ivy League schools do not offer athletic scholarships, so the thought of full tuition made the plane tickets and camp registrations seem modest by comparison. Andrew performed very well at both camps, but neither program was inclined to take a chance on him because of his size. Brian Earl, former player and brand new assistant coach at Princeton wrote and said, "I watched Andrew pretty closely on Tuesday and Thursday and thought he played well. He competes, shoots well, and more importantly hits the big shots. The biggest negative is his size and that keeps him below some of the other players we are recruiting in his spot right now." Later in the summer Coach Earl's counterpart at Columbia, Andrew Theokas, wrote, "We were all very impressed with Andrew, and we feel that if he matures physically he has the potential to be a Division I basketball player." Unless the pituitary gland suddenly kicked into high gear, however, Andrew appeared unlikely to get an

Ivy League education, and I was relieved of the anxiety of wondering how to finance one.

That did not remove other nearer-term basketball-related financial considerations. Andrew's AAU team was a group of inner-city kids without the means to make the trip to tournaments in Indianapolis and Louisville in the Midwest, or the bigger one in Las Vegas. I swallowed hard and then reached for my credit card. For the most part I was pleased to be able to help. The coaches and kids were grateful for the opportunity to do something that otherwise would not have been possible. It gave them something special to look forward to doing and a reason to work hard and stay focused all summer long. Everybody wanted to impress the college scouts. What bothered me, however, was a question that poked like a pin: "Why was I doing this, anyway?" My conscience was being probed, and I worried there might be a bigger price to pay than what could be measured in dollars and cents.

Of course, I was trying to help Andrew. Nobody deserved success more than he did. That salve appeased my conscience a little. Questions nevertheless lingered. In helping him to accomplish his goals I wondered whether I was undermining all that I valued most. I had not completely forgotten that the main reason I was president of Concordia University was because I believed passionately in the mission of our school. Moreover, I believed in the significance and even superiority of Christian higher education and doubted whether the experience could come close to being replicated just anywhere, even at an Ivy League school. In fact, I feared that at most places the aims and objectives intrinsic and inherent in Christian higher education were often deliberately and systematically undermined. Why would I aid and abet that process by encouraging my own son possibly to attend such a place just to play basketball? Understandably, Andrew was uninterested in enrolling at the university where his father was president. As president I also recognized that parents should avoid endeavoring to make their child's choice of a college for them. However, parents play a key part in helping to define the range of options from which their sons and daughters decide. I began to fear that I was failing in a parental responsibility that from my own experience I regarded as one of my most sacred duties:

> "What does it profit a man to gain the whole world but to lose his soul?" For me basketball was a conduit to Christ, a means of moving me into a Christian setting and toward a life-changing experience. How will it work for Andrew? What would it profit him to play Division I if basketball was not a way to grow in faith and be encouraged in service? I have always believed that the college choice is a pivotal one in that the experience can have a profound shaping impact on a young person. Andrew is grounded. He has a strong faith. But, I pray that his collegiate experience would build up rather than draw away from Christ.

Qualms of conscience notwithstanding, the airline tickets to Las Vegas were already purchased, and there was no turning back. "Poor kid," I wrote in my journal a couple of days into our trip, "he works hard all spring and summer to get ready for this and then breaks out with shingles all over his right side just before the tournament." Andrew could barely lift his right arm on account of the painful sores and scars. His performance also suffered, and needless to say he was devastated. "This trip is costing me a fortune," I lamented, "like those gamblers on the floor I am rolling the dice and coming up empty." The Las Vegas excursion certainly did nothing to reinforce Jefferson's definition of luck. The harder we worked, the more only bad luck seemed to follow. I wrote, "If this was his big chance he gave it all he had but came up short." That, along with the fact that he came up short in stature, sent a fairly clear signal, "Andrew will not likely be on anybody's short list among Division I schools next year."

I pondered further at some length:

I have wrestled with this a lot. It strikes me as unfair almost. His size, his diabetes, and then throw in a last minute bout with shingles. Is it a story about overcoming obstacles? Time will tell. But, maybe we should be reading it differently and interpreting it all more accurately. If Andrew wants to keep pushing and working toward a goal that he may not be able to attain, that is not such a bad thing. He should reach high.

But, what about me? How do I help him as a parent? What should my counsel be? Should I mind my own business and, as they say in Las Vegas, let the chips fall where they may?

I have prayed long and hard and have asked God to help us. My faith is tested and my trust has been shaken. I feel like God is working at cross purposes here. Of course, that is true. He allows us crosses of various sorts for purposes that are of His own counsel. I would like to get on the same page. The Lord will, I hope and trust, help to lead us there.

Andrew says he can't catch a break. For the most part I agree (although in the broader scheme he has had many breaks and blessings). But, he is being thwarted from reaching his goal. I don't blame God. At the same time, the path toward Andrew's aspirations has not been easy. Indeed, it seems that a series of divine detours is leading him a different direction. Where?

I finished the day's journal entry with this prayer:

Abba Father—I am a dedicated dad who loves his children. If your love for us is even more than my love for my kids, then I am impressed. Help me to believe that, to trust that, to experience that. Help my children to believe, know, trust, and experience your love for them in Christ.

The following day, our next-to-last in Las Vegas, Andrew had 30 points, including nine three-pointers in a losing effort. Since we were by now in the consolation bracket in an elimination game there were only a few parents in the stands. The scouts were elsewhere. That evening Andrew hooked up with his friend, Jake Barnett, on the strip. A coach from North Carolina-Greensboro approached them and knew them both by name. Later he texted our coach and acknowledged that Andrew was "an unbelievable shooter" but they had other players like that on their team and would use scholarships somewhere else.

The trip puzzled me. What if Andrew's breakout game had come a day earlier in front of all those coaches? What if he had not broken out with shingles in the first place? "Who knows?" What was clear was that Andrew was getting lots of attention from Division III schools. "Maybe that is where he will end up." The summer blitz ended; it was time for a little reprieve. "For now we can let it rest awhile—follow up if anybody contacts us, but otherwise just take a break."

Rest never came. Andrew's considerable exposure at summer camps and on the AAU circuit did, in fact, stimulate lots of interest. Overall he played very well, and his consistent performance drew attention from coaches across the country—nearly all of them Division III coaches. At first Andrew enjoyed the phone calls and letters and all of the complimentary comments from small college mentors who expressed their desire to have Andrew become a part of their programs. Since Concordia is a Division III institution I am aware of how strenuously coaches have to exert themselves in order to attract athletes. Lacking the benefit of athletic scholarships to entice kids they want to recruit, Division III coaching staffs work doubly hard to establish relationships and tout the distinct benefits of their schools and being part of their teams. Letters, texts, e-mails, and phone calls—to his cell and our home number—were incessant for several weeks.

I expressed to Andrew my expectation that he should be courteous and cordial when approached by people who were interested in him as a student athlete. Telephone etiquette and diplomatic discourse were lessons learned early. The balance between leaving options open and politely indicating that he was not interested took awhile to perfect. Once the volume became too much to handle—two or three coaches called every single night as school started—he gradually began to shift from "keeping an open mind" to "thanks, but no thanks." All the while he was not so secretly hoping the Division I opportunity might yet materialize, but he also knew it might never happen. Those calls never came.

A few of the Division III schools were too intriguing simply to ignore. We visited the University of Chicago and New York University, both world-class institutions, and both in the University Athletic Association, which is a conference of selective private universities from around the country. Of the two, Andrew preferred NYU. The campus, in the heart of Greenwich Village in New York City, was remarkable.

The coaches described Andrew as their "top perimeter prospect." He liked everything about the place, he told me, except that it was not Division I. In the end he never bothered to apply.

The Division III school that most interested me besides Concordia, which I knew was not going to be Andrew's choice, was Wheaton College in Illinois. Wheaton enjoys a distinguished reputation for academic excellence and is widely recognized as one of the premier Christian colleges in the country. Before Wheaton's coach, Bill Harris, ever attempted to contact Andrew, he called me to ask for permission to recruit my son. He understood that I was the president of Concordia University and did not wish to put me in an awkward position, so he requested my approval before initiating any conversation with Andrew. I was impressed by this gesture, which struck me as above and beyond the call of duty. Being a college president was not leveraged to help Andrew in this case. Coach Harris wanted to be sure that it was not a hindrance.

A few weeks later Coach Harris and Nate Frank, his top assistant, asked for the chance to meet with us in our home. I anticipated their visit with a little trepidation and wrote in my journal, "Tomorrow two coaches from Wheaton College are making a home visit and will take Andrew to dinner. Wheaton, of course, is the premier evangelical school … it would take some explaining, I guess. But, if it is a good fit then I would rather have him at Wheaton than most of the other places that expressed interest." If Andrew was going to attend a Division III school and a Christian college, most folks who knew us would wonder why he didn't just go to Concordia, and if not ours then why not one of the other Concordia colleges and universities that were affiliated with us? In fact, we visited Concordia in St. Paul, Minnesota, which is actually a

Division II school. Andrew left with the distinct impression that they welcomed him more as a courtesy to me than because they were truly interested in him. In any event, I was not sure how my Lutheran family, friends, and colleagues would react to Wheaton.

The next evening Coach Harris and Coach Frank sat down with us in our living room. After getting better acquainted they extolled the virtues of Wheaton College for an hour before taking Andrew to Applebee's for dinner. Once they left I wrote that Andrew was "favorably impressed and eager to visit campus." Tammy and I also "were impressed by their presentation and solid commitment to Christian faith, excellent academics, and good basketball." Maybe no Concordia had any chance to emerge as Andrew's preference, but my predisposition toward Christian higher education was certainly reinforced by the Wheaton visit. "The farther we go along," I wrote, "the more convinced I am that the spirituality piece must not be marginalized in the process." From that point on I began rooting for Wheaton to be Andrew's choice.

Wheaton was rooting for Andrew too. Almost every single game his senior year, home and away, Wheaton sent a coach to watch. Even when Milwaukee Lutheran played a game in Florida, a trip for which they had planned and raised funds for a couple of years, Wheaton sent an alum and former player to represent them. After a game in January in which Andrew uncharacteristically found himself in foul trouble and played only limited minutes, I told Wheaton assistant Owen Handy that we should reimburse him for his mileage. He braved snow, cold, and Chicago traffic to make the three-hour trip to be in attendance. He replied that Wheaton was not evaluating whether Andrew could play for them. They came to support him and to show their interest. The last regular season game of the year was at Port Washington, another hour north and that much farther away for Coach Harris, who battled blizzard conditions and left his sweetheart of a wife at home on Valentine's Day just to watch Andrew play. Following that appearance and heroic effort I was sold and was definitely pulling for Wheaton.

Andrew, however, was leaning toward Valparaiso University. Valpo was simultaneously attractive and complicated both for Andrew and for me. At over six thousand students, Concordia University Wisconsin, where I was president, was the largest Lutheran college in North America. Valpo, on the other hand, was probably the best known Lutheran university in the country. By most any reckoning Valpo also enjoyed a reputation for superior academics. The northwest Indiana school was consistently rated with rave reviews and near the top of its category by *US News and World Report* in the popular annual "America's Best Colleges" edition of the magazine. Both Lutheran and also well-regarded were surely good places to start.

Tammy's mother, Andrew's Grandma Saleska was a Valpo alumna. She met my father-in-law, John, on campus when he spent a summer there doing graduate studies. Their son and Tammy's younger brother, Thad, was also an alum and former VU tennis player. Family connections added to our interest.

Valpo was probably most famous for its basketball program. Even better still, Coach Homer Drew was a devout Christian man whose faith was meaningfully integrated into his coaching and his work with young men. In 1998 the team had "one shining moment" of particular note when Coach Drew's son, Bryce, hit a miraculous last second shot to advance Valpo in the NCAA tournament toward a Sweet Sixteen appearance. Bryce, who was now an assistant to his father, played several seasons in the NBA. Every March, however, what Valpo now simply refers to as "The Shot" is replayed as one of the NCAA tournament's most memorable highlights, and it remains both Bryce's and the school's main claim to fame. The Hoosier state's passion for hoops is legendary, and Valparaiso University took its basketball tradition very seriously, and the legendary coach took his Christian faith seriously. What could be better?

Not academic prestige, nor Lutheran heritage, nor family history, nor basketball tradition, nor Coach Drew's sterling reputation were of primary significance to Andrew. What mattered more was that Homer Drew extended him an invitation to join the team and experience a Division I basketball program as a "walk-on."

Coach Drew and I spoke on the phone soon after our return from Las Vegas. It was a continuation of a discussion that we had begun before the summer. My intention had been to reach out to him, along with other coaches at mid-major universities, but Homer preempted my contact with a call of his own to me. For all of my meticulous effort to market Andrew's potential, Homer became aware of him on a tip from Valpo's president, who had chatted with my mother-in-law at an alumni event. She unabashedly boasted about her grandson, and the president passed along Andrew's name to his coach. So much for leveraging my position to have an impact; Grandma Saleska evidently had more clout than I did!

Being a walk-on would not be all glitter and glamour. Homer indicated that he had no available scholarships for the next year. In addition, he mentioned that there was not much chance of advancing from being a walk-on to a scholarship player. In his nineteen years of coaching that had happened on only one previous occasion. Nevertheless, Homer said Andrew could be part of the team. The benefits included daily workouts and coachs' instruction, as well as suiting up for contests at home and away, which meant traveling for road games. If Andrew was determined to be on a Division I basketball team, Valpo was the one school in the country offering him the opportunity—albeit with no promise of actually setting foot on the floor or competing in any meaningful minutes.

Why would Homer Drew offer Andrew even this much virtually sight unseen? Surely a coach who was nearing six hundred career victories did not achieve such success merely following the advice of grandmas, even ones who were among Valpo's interested alumni. It was no reach to suspect that Coach Drew was aware that my name was being circulated as a candidate to become the next president of Valparaiso University. The search to replace the retiring leader was just getting underway, but rumors were already floating around that I might be in line for the job. Coach Drew had too much tact to make any overt connections between the invitation to Andrew and the possibility of my own candidacy. Both topics, however, came up during our conversation. As we prepared to hang up, Homer said he "hoped both Ferrys would end up at Valpo," and invited us to visit campus, meet with him, and attend a practice session. If my current position did little to further Andrew's chances to land a Division I scholarship, at least the possibility of becoming president at Valpo was enough for its coach to allow him to walk on.

We took Homer up on his offer and made a trip to Valpo. Reminders of "The Shot" decorated the basketball offices, and the presence of Bryce Drew himself in one of those offices brought Valpo's glorious past into the present. While he was mostly treated like a regular recruit, we both sensed from our conversation with Homer that the coach felt Andrew's biggest contribution to the program might be as a manager. Unfazed, Andrew believed Homer would be pleasantly surprised and won over once he saw what he was capable of contributing. After our brief visit I recorded impressions of our day at Valpo that proved to be prophetic—for both of us:

> If I were to guess, I'd say this is probably where Andrew will be a year from now. Lots could happen between now and then, but I think this is what Andrew has been looking for. Even without the scholarship there is a window of opportunity and he will take advantage. It will be a huge climb to have a meaningful role in the program, but Andrew does not lack confidence. He would be determined to prove himself.

> By way of contrast, I really do not see myself here a year from now. I will do a video interview next week with the head of the search firm, but I just don't have the feeling that Valpo is the place for me. That could change, of course, and I am not ruling anything out just yet. But, I see Andrew here and not the rest of us.

The presidential search process continued until just before Christmas, and I stayed engaged until its conclusion with a very public campus interview of the finalists. The field had been culled from hundreds to just three. The on-campus experience affirmed my feeling that it was not the right place for me, nor was I the man for Valpo. Secretly, part of the reason I hung in so long was because I liked the idea of being so close to Valpo basketball, especially if my son was on the team. Ironically, Andrew claimed that he would not enroll if I were president there. I didn't believe him. In the end the issue was moot. My leverage lost, I wondered whether Homer wanted to renege on his invitation to a walk-on from whom he expected essentially nothing. He didn't. He wouldn't—that was not Homer's style. To me, Homer Drew was the best thing about Valparaiso University, and I was pleased Andrew would be mentored by such a fine man whether or not he actually appeared in a game his freshman year.

Before his freshman year in college began, of course, Andrew's senior year in high school remained. It was easier for me to keep my composure than it had been the year before because Andrew was exceptional most of the season. I had my moments; craziness is not a condition easily cured. While no less intense, for the most part I minded my manners and was better behaved.

His performance on the court generated interest in the struggles that he experienced off the court. The local Fox television affiliate did a special interest segment on Andrew's battle with diabetes which aired several times. The *Milwaukee Journal Sentinel* published a feature article about Andrew with the headline, "Gauging success by the numbers: Guard attacks diabetes, foes with great determination." His photograph, tongue hanging out á la Michael Jordan, shows him poised to fire his patented jump shot. Sportswriter Anthony Witrado wrote about Andrew's extraordinary halftime routine and the necessity of constant finger pricks to test his blood sugar level. He also described the respect Andrew enjoyed from his coaches and teammates. "The kid is such a competitor," said Coach Jason Moesch, "I think if we was feeling weird, he might not tell us because he'd have to come out." Witrado continued:

Diabetes is with him forever. There is no cure. The disease has changed the way he attacks life and the game. Ferry learned to better focus and pay attention in counting his carbohydrate or sugar intake daily. It is a work ethic and discipline that translates to the gym.

"It helps with everything, basketball and school," Ferry said. 'Everything I do now has to have a purpose, whether it is eating or making a move on the court."

Ferry stood 5 feet 2 inches and weighed 90 pounds as a freshman and was a three-point specialist. But after last season, he had a ridiculous growth spurt, shooting up 4 inches to 5-11, although he likes to smile and call himself a 6-footer.

With body growth came skill development. He improved his ball-handling, defense, and one-on-one game. Now Ferry is an all-around player and earning college interest. But, those around him say he is an all-around person, not just a ballplayer.

"If I had a son," Moesch said, "he'd be the kind of son I'd want. That's just the person he is."

Andrew was my son, and when his senior season ended I wrote reflectively, much as Chris Peterson wrote to me after my final game at Jefferson:

The Sun came up today, and last night's punctuation was a period and not an exclamation mark. We lost to Brown Deer 87–72. Milwaukee Lutheran's guys played hard but could never close the gap. For his part (just like all season long) Andrew was terrific. He scored 26 points despite tremendous defensive pressure. The team's final record was 12–10—about where they belonged. Andrew, on the other hand, was anything but average. He was outstanding. All year as a basketball player he continually exceeded my expectations … .

He has been an inspiration. Yesterday he was invited to be the 'Youth Ambassador' for the American Diabetes Association. People have been touched by his story … .

A hug at half court after the game brought me very close to tears. I told Andrew that I was proud of him and that this was not so much the end of something as the beginning of what comes next. What comes next? Like Andrew, I'd rather not think about it just now.

For my part, I want a little while to savor what has been one of the most enjoyable experiences in my life. If, as I suspect, I have been looking for this as some way to compensate for my own athletic underachievement, I am more than fulfilled.

But, that is hardly the point. This is not about me, it is about Andrew. My only real connection to this is as a proud parent who is grateful for this and all of God's blessings.

I wasn't lucky, I was blessed, and all of the hard work was worth whatever was expended to get to this point. Mick Jagger put it this way: "You can't always get what you want, but if you try sometimes, you just might find, you get what you need."

"NIGHT FEVER"
CHAPTER 7

September 1977–July 1978—*Saturday Night Fever* was all the rage that year. John Travolta played Tony Manero, a troubled Brooklyn kid whose otherwise woefully depressing life was gladly laid to the side and temporarily forgotten on Saturday nights. When he appeared at the local discotheque Tony entered a sanctuary from his struggles, his haven from hard times. Through the disco's door he stepped into a magical place that bore almost no resemblance to the harsh world outside. Here he could escape, at least for awhile.

Inside, the atmosphere was enhanced by the rotating glitter ball that hung conspicuously above the center of the dance floor. As the ball was put into motion, its mirrored surface reflected beams from colored strobes. Myriad spots of light scattered and hypnotically spun on the walls, on the floor, and on the ceiling all around the room. Tony, arrayed in his three-piece white suit offset by his open-collared black shirt, held one hand akimbo while with the other he reached up and pointed the index finger skyward. The musical soundtrack of the Bee Gees pulsated as he rhythmically executed his disco-booted footwork with tightly choreographed precision. The command performance kept all eyes glued with rapt attention in Tony's direction. Eventually the momentarily mesmerized crowd regained its wits and lined up to join Tony on the floor. Following his lead, each dancer was as familiar as the next with every step and gesture as they moved feet and hands, legs and arms together in unison. Night fever, night fever—they knew how to do it!

The film was a smash hit, and the songs recorded for *Saturday Night Fever* became the bestselling soundtrack of all time. Disco music suddenly became wildly popular, and teens showed up in droves to do their best John Travolta imitations at disco joints surfacing across the country.

Not surprisingly, no disco place sprung up in Winfield. Like Tony Manero, however, I relied on weekends to provide brief relief from the rest of my melancholy life. "Getting out of Dodge," was the way I described looking for a way to escape Winfield for a few hours. Comparing Winfield to Dodge City probably was not a compliment to either town. The best remedy for my own Saturday night fever, presuming basketball did not interfere and supposing I could convince Reed or Erik to drive, was the forty-five-minute trip to Wichita—the closest thing to civilization that Kansas had to offer. It sometimes took a little arm-twisting, and when all else failed I was persistent to the point of offering to pay for gas with the $10 bill that Billie had generously included inside the envelope along with her most recent letter. Usually that was sufficient persuasion for my equally bored buddies, even though Reed wasn't much for dancing, and Erik was more of a rock-

and-roll than disco kind of guy. For my part, I was sufficiently smitten with boogie fever in high school to invest in a pair of disco boots of my own. A few disco albums were added to the record collection to play on my stereo during the week in order to heighten anticipation of the weekend ahead. Saturday night in Wichita, Kansas! Life didn't get any better than this—at least not during the first semester of my freshman year.

Pogo's, Wichita's favorite hangout for kids feverish for Saturday night diversion, had its last chance for one final dance at midnight. Up to that point I was not exactly a dancing machine. Too shy and self-conscious to get the nerve actually to ask somebody to join me under the glitter ball on the dance floor, I lived in an illusory world where I imagined some disco darling would invite me out of the seat I had occupied most of the evening. "Dream on," I chided myself, but, with nothing better to do we stayed until they closed the place down anyway. After a late-night fourth meal at McDonald's, a culinary option not yet available in Winfield, we made the dark, desolate drive back to campus.

Tired and yawning as we walked into Rehwinkel at two o'clock in the morning, we were serenaded down the hallway by yet another Commodores' song blaring from Vince and Scott's room. The decibel level was in blatant disregard for quiet hours rules in effect at that time of night, but the music didn't bother me. "Brick House" probably shook the walls of our limestone dormitory a few minutes earlier as we drove into the parking lot, but the last song on the album was a softer ballad by Lionel Richie that struck just the right chord with me. I was soothed by the idea that despite staying up long and late with my Saturday night fever I could now look forward to something "Easy like a Sunday morning."

Most other Rehwinkel residents did not slumber away Sunday mornings like I did. I caught up with them around noon at the Campus Center, where by far the best meal of the week was prepared and served by the St. John's College kitchen staff. Saturday night's McDonald's would tie me over long enough to do without breakfast, but missing Sunday's lunch was never a serious consideration. The spread was always much too good to miss, and, besides, sleeping until midday was long enough even for somebody as lazy as I. Roast beef, fried chicken, mashed potatoes and gravy, fresh rolls, and delicious desserts were always on the menu. The cooks prided themselves on their Sunday noon meal, and their effort endeared them to every student on campus.

Those good feelings lasted only until Sunday's supper, when leftovers from the previous week were warmed up and served. There was, of course, a reason they had leftovers in the first place, and the reheated version was no more appealing the second time around. All the more reason, we realized, to take advantage of the noon meal. If I got out of bed a few minutes early I knew that I could throw on my sweats and be among the first in line to eat when the serving station opened. On the other hand, if I waited too long I risked arriving after the brunt of the campus population, which arrived at the Campus Center each week en masse.

If they were Catholics it would have been after Mass. Instead the rest of the Johnnies gradually ambled over after regular worship services dismissed from the local Lutheran church. Trinity Lutheran was within short walking distance, located only a couple of blocks off campus. Most St. John's students favored the 10:30 late service. The easiest thing about Sunday morning was to tell which kids rolled over and went back to sleep while the others got out of bed, put on Sunday clothes, and went to church. Showing up at the mess hall looking very much a mess myself, I was among the more slovenly dressed ones who waited for lunch at the front of the line. Watching the others through the windows of the Campus Center as they walked together across the front lawn of St. John's College toward us unkempt kids, I couldn't help but wonder what else distinguished them from me. Indeed, more than curious, I was also a little envious. Even though I was going to get lunch before they did, and the smell wafting from the kitchen suggested it was going to taste good, I knew that I was hungry for something they seemed already to have. Would I have to give up more than sleep to get some? How much of my life would have to change?

As I became a little better acquainted, I decided that my new class-mates might not be so peculiar after all. In fact, they were lots like me in many ways. They listened to the same music. They wore the same sorts of clothes. They had the same haircuts. They missed their friends and family back home. They liked to get letters. They didn't want to study for class. They skipped stuff on a shingle for breakfast. They hated losing games by monumental margins. They even went to Wichita on weekends, because I saw some of them at Pogo's. Many of the John-nies did both disco and also the Divine Service without missing a beat. Somehow they managed to navigate their way around both worlds with relative Saturday night and Sunday morning ease. My stereotypes and initial impressions required review as I came to realize that in lots of ways we were more similar than I wanted to admit. The most obvious difference, as far as I could tell, was they went to church while I slept in. Of course, I knew it was not that simple. My honest analysis, although

I was slow to accept the fact, was that these Johnnies were not really that strange. Maybe I was the odd one out. I began to detect that they had a dimension in their lives that I lacked in my own.

To me the fever for Saturday nights and easy Sunday mornings had little in common except that one led to the other. My expectation was that Wichita's disco and Winfield's church were also vastly different. Pogo's and Trinity had to be more worlds apart than a mere forty-five-minute drive would suggest. Had I set my alarm to get out of bed and covertly snuck over for the late service one Sunday morning, and if I were alert enough after the long, late Saturday night before, I might have uncovered some unexpected similarities between the two.

The ambiance in the Lutheran church was also otherworldly. It was that way by design, so that when people walked through the church doors there was an immediate and unmistakable awareness that this place was distinct from any other. Replacing the glitter ball there hung a giant cross spot lit and conspicuously suspended over the center, not of the dance floor but of the altar area. Candles burned and tossed flickering light that was clearly visible from the front to the balcony in back. From that same balcony, familiar musical selections, including some of the most sung songs in the history of the world, were played on the majestic pipe organ. While there was no confusing him for John Travolta, standing before the rest and pointing them heavenward was a man decked out in white garb, his black shirt with buttoned-up collar beneath. He led the others through a tightly choreographed order of service, and everybody followed his lead. They were completely comfortable, after many weeks of rehearsal, with every single step to take along the way. Eventually, the cast of congregants lined up to join him around the altar beneath the cross with knees uniformly bent and hands universally folded. Everyone spoke, sang, and moved in unison until it was time to go home—or to go get some lunch.

For the Johnnies who gathered, Trinity was a sanctuary from struggles, a haven from hard times, a place to escape. Here was a weekend refuge without a cover charge and somewhere to go that required no money for gas. I could have just walked inside, but my shadow didn't darken the door.

Counting on one hand the number of times I attended church services growing up would have left a few fingers still unused. Billie occasionally dropped off my sister and me at the local Methodist Church's Sunday school and picked us up an hour later to bring us home. One morning she drove us in my brother Bill's old VW Bug, which backfired—loudly-every time she shifted gears. Unknown to us as we pulled out of the driveway, a squirrel that had fallen to its untimely and unhappy demise from either our crabapple tree or a telephone wire overhead was lodged on to the front fender. Only after we started down the road and its tail began to flop in the breeze did we even become aware of the poor critter's misfortune. As Billie pulled in front of the church, Volkswagen backfiring and dead squirrel dangling, my sister and I rushed from the car to the church door hoping to remain unseen. Admittedly, the whole scene was a little unusual, but skipping church services after Sunday school was not. After eighth grade, Sunday school became a thing of my past. By the time I started high school at Jefferson the pattern of late night Saturdays and sleeping in Sundays was well entrenched. I took it easy.

Church and religion were almost never topics of conversation either within our family or between me and my Jefferson friends. To say that I was uninterested in God, however, could not have been further from the truth, no matter how far from truth I might have been. For example, a social studies class on the "world's great religions" that I took in high school was among my favorites, and I aced the course—much to the teacher, Max Snyder's, surprise. As he handed me back my first exam, an errorless multiple choice test on Hinduism and Buddhism, Mr. Snyder said, "No offense, but I didn't think that you looked that bright." I wasn't particularly offended; I just figured that if my favorite singer and songwriter Cat Stevens thought enough of Buddha to name an album after him maybe I should learn a little about him myself:

> They called him Guatama Buddha, long time ago. He turned the world to order, don't you know. He used to sit knowing, long time ago, where you and me were going .... .

If Buddha did actually know where I was going then he might have been even more astonished than Max Snyder to find me perusing the shelves of Jefferson's library one day looking for something to read. I serendipitously stumbled across Herman Hesse's *Siddhartha*. The fact that this was a classic eluded me. A couple of things did intrigue me about the novel, however, as I judged the book by its cover. First, it wasn't very long. Second, the story was set in India around the time of Buddha and described the spiritual odyssey of Siddhartha and a quest for enlightenment that led him various directions to numerous places. Though I had rarely picked up a book in high school, especially if it was not assigned, I devoured Hesse's story in a couple of evenings. Thereafter I fancied myself, if not a full-fledged, modern-day Siddhartha, then at least something like Cat Stevens, who sang about being "On the Road to Find Out."

Inspired, I actually took notes and studied hard for world's great religions, never missing a single question on any test or quiz in Mr.

Snyder's class for the entire course. Looks can be deceiving, and I defied his initial impression of me. My goal, however, was less to impress him than to consider in more depth and detail ideas that were making an impression on me.

In the same song in which he sang about Buddha, Cat Stevens also sang about Jesus: "They used to call him Jesus, long time ago. They're still calling him Jesus, don't you know. They crossed the wood and hanged him, long time ago. They still misunderstand him, those who don't know." While I didn't really dwell on the point of the lyric, it occurred to me that I might be among those who still misunderstood Jesus. Sometimes I thought about him, and occasionally muttered a silent prayer to him under my breath before I fell asleep at night. My interest was stimulated during my last year of Sunday school in eigth grade, when our teacher took us to see the recently released film *Jesus Christ Superstar.* One of the Peterson brothers owned the album with all the songs from the movie, and I borrowed it and listened until I knew each one by heart. In one of those songs, the disciples were aroused from sleep as Jesus was dragged from them to be hanged on the crossed wood. Even they couldn't understand, "what's the buzz?" or figure out "what's a happening." The significance of Jesus mostly buzzed right by me. Periodically my curiosity was piqued. Once in awhile I was also a little afraid.

Conversation about Christianity was not completely muted during my high school years. A girl who I dated from Jefferson tried literally to "scare the hell out of me." She was on the Pom Pon, squad which aligned well with her true passion—the girl was a diehard disco dancer. She was also a dyed-in-the-wool Roman Catholic who repeatedly threatened that were I to die I was a sure-fire candidate for hellfire because I had never been baptized. What if she was right? A couple of soapbox preachers who cornered me in downtown Denver one evening left a similar impression. I was cruising the city blocks along Sixteenth Street with a carload of guys and a sizeable portion of the teenaged population of the metropolitan area when traffic grinded to a halt—too many cars in too confined a space. The zealots took advantage of gridlock and preached an impromptu sermon. Nobody listened to them except me, and while I was not exactly spellbound, I was at least courteous. Evidently they noticed I was paying attention because when they finished their message they prayed for me on the spot. It was Saturday night and I was looking for amusement, not searching for Jesus, but they made me drive home wondering whether I was cruising straight down the path to eternal damnation.

Now at St. John's I found myself surrounded by people mostly my own age apparently with inside information on the ultimate final exam. I may have had no clue but was not about to ask any of them for help sorting it out. From the beginning I warily kept up my guard and was determined to maintain arm's length between myself and the Johnnies. Yet, someone might easily have mistaken me for Shakespeare's character from *Hamlet,* which we read in Coach Skov's English class:"he doth protest too much, methinks." The more I insisted to my mother, my friends, or even to myself that I wanted to switch off all of the religion stuff going on around me, the more actually I yearned for answers. Along with everything else squished into the Granada, I brought from home with me both enough curiosity and also sufficient concern at least to ask and explore. Cat Stevens described it best:

Well I left my happy home to see what I could find out. I left my folks and friends with the aim to clear my mind out. Well I hit the rowdy road and many kinds I met there. Many stories told me of the way to get there

So on and on I go, the seconds tick the time out. There's so much left to know, and I'm on the road to find out.

For me that road headed east along I-70, veered south at Salina through Wichita, crossed the Walnut River into Winfield, turned left on College Street off Ninth Avenue, and on to the campus of St. John's College.

Reed and I occasionally attended morning chapel services in the Meyer Hall Auditorium right from the very start. Chapel, for some reason, just seemed lots less daunting than Sunday worship services. Since it was right on campus and part of the daily routine, very little extra effort was required. You just had to show up and sit there for twenty minutes. Once upon a time these brief meditations were mandatory for Johnnies. In the old days seats were assigned and attendance was taken. Thankfully, that was no longer true, but students were still pestered to be present. So, I went.

The first morning of the fall semester the college president, Dr. Michael Stelmachowicz, spoke on the theme for the 1977–1978 school year, "Taste and See that the Lord is Good." His message to us was that daily chapel was the place where our spirit was fed and that it was just as crucial as the physical nourishment that we received for our bodies each day in the Campus Center. Don't skip breakfast, and don't skip chapel. He also reminded us of the St. John's motto emblazoned on the official college seal which read, "The Fear of the Lord is the Beginning of Wisdom." Fear I knew, so I assumed that I must be on the right track. The invitation to taste and see the goodness of the Lord allayed apprehensions a bit, and showing up for chapel once in a while was an innocuous enough way to sample what St. John's was all about without biting off more than I cared to chew.

For the many difficulties it presented to me, the distance from Denver did make it easier to take a taste of Christianity without any family or friends besides Reed looking over my shoulder. I certainly didn't want anybody to think that I was taking Jesus too seriously. They might worry that I had changed or suspect that I was no longer the guy that I used to be or imagine that I had gone off the deep end. Still, I was never good at secrets, and I didn't want to keep my exploration totally to myself. It might have been less onerous for me to tell her that I was out drinking and carousing every night if it were true—lots of college students did that stuff—but I wrote to Billie anyway to give her a heads up about my spiritual journey. Remaining suspicious of the overt, overemphatic Christian influence in my classes and elsewhere on campus, I continued to protest—methinks too much. Nevertheless, I also acknowledged, "The religion is not all bad. In fact, it is good. The school helps promote spiritual growth, and you couldn't avoid it even if you wanted to." I didn't want to. There were still things that bugged me about the folks at St. Johns. "I don't approve of some of their narrow-minded philosophies," but at the same time I acknowledged "strong faith and worship is now important to me." I explained to Billie why I felt as I did. "There is much to be thankful for and God deserves that thanks. It's really the least I can do."

How much of "the least that can I do" could be done at St. John's? Most people on campus were Lutheran, but I wasn't, and that was a bit of a problem. Comfortable distance was still a strong objective. I wasn't one of them. So, where did I fit? Maybe I was not really a Siddharthian seeker either, as romantic as that seemed. My guess was, if anything,

I must have been a Methodist. There was a Methodist church a few blocks north on College Street between St. John's and Southwestern College. Billie may have been relieved to learn the incident with the dead squirrel had not completely seared my soul and soured me on Methodist churches forever—not that she ever went to church herself. She was probably taken aback a bit when I wrote to tell her, "Reed and I went to the Methodist Church last Sunday." And that was not all. "We also attend chapel services here on campus daily." What I failed to mention still lingered in the back of my mind, where I continued to hear my Roman Catholic girlfriend warning me about the perils of not being baptized. While I was dabbling in Christianity anyway, why not get that detail finally addressed? In my next letter I informed Billie:

> Tomorrow afternoon I have an appointment with the Rev. at Grace
> Methodist. At that time I will find out about baptism and becoming
> an official member of the Methodist church. Baptism is symbolic
> of accepting Christ into your life and, as you know, is something
> I think I've wanted for a long time.

My guess was this news would probably throw my parents for a loop. Not that they would disapprove necessarily, but there were sure to be some questions swirling in their minds. I wanted to urge them not to suspect that I was undergoing too radical a change in my life. Indeed, my desire to be baptized was motivated as much by fear as by faith. The Methodist preacher sought to assure me that God's acceptance of me was not contingent upon anything I might do, including agreeing to be baptized, but that divine love was solely a gift of grace. That sounded great, I tasted and saw that it was good, but just in case my old girlfriend knew as much about the disposition of the deity as she did about disco dancing, I didn't want to take any chances. I planned to be baptized just to play it safe. However, to let Billie and Lefty know that this baptism thing was really not such a big deal to me, I wrote:

> Don't worry about me becoming a Jesus Freak or anything because I'm not. I have an open mind, and I'll never be like almost everybody else around this place is. But I'm grateful and have faith so I may as well show it.

"Jesus freak"—that was the reputation I probably feared most. If too many people back home got wind of some of the things that I was up to in Kansas they might blow it all out of proportion. They themselves might even freak out. How would others react? Did they even have to know? To my great relief, Billie was untroubled by my plan. On the Saturday before my baptism she wrote me a letter: "I wish I could be with you tomorrow at church. I'm very pleased you are going to be baptized and very proud of your decision." My mom, at least, was not worried that her son had lost his identity seeking to save his soul. On the Monday afterward I wrote her a letter that crossed with hers in the mail. With underwhelming description I offered a brief account of the event: "I was baptized yesterday. It was very nice and certainly a worthwhile experience. Everything went well. Reed was there as were a few Lutheran friends." To assure Billie that not very much had actually changed, I also wrote, "It was hard getting up Sunday for the baptism because we were out late Saturday night." Suddenly Sunday morning was no longer quite so easy, but baptism's splash did little to cool my Saturday night fever.

Gradually, however, the fever began to break. "Sunday morning fervor" eventually ensued. There was no blinding light, the earth never shook. It was neither dazzling nor dramatic. Subtle and nuanced describe it better. But, somewhere along the way, and at no specific point in particular, my quest and my questions led to the place where the folks at St. John's suggested that I look all along. Indeed, it was not a place at all but a person—Jesus. As my desire to learn more about Jesus intensified, my preoccupation with other things, including basketball, began to diminish. Given that basketball was my sole reason for coming to Winfield in the first place, the recognition that my dream was unraveling was difficult to accept. I struggled to find the words to describe what I was feeling, but that did not stop me from thinking my way through the situation in a letter home:

> I really think this could be my last year of playing. I'm slowly losing enthusiasm and am interested in broadening my horizons. Perhaps a better season and/or a more optimistic outlook for next year might persuade me to stick with it longer, but things aren't going that way now. It is not the same as high school basketball at all. Practices are too easy, and players are too apathetic. The coach is prejudiced in favor of his son and more than a little off beat … .
> It is very disappointing, but I realize that I can't play forever. It is not like Rick and Chris; for one thing they are more talented, for another basketball is their whole life. I love to play, but I am tired of all the practicing and work involved, especially when I have other things to do that could be more important and relevant in my life.

I was searching for something more important and relevant. The emotional trials and travails, first of homesickness to the point of near neurosis, followed by a basketball debacle of unprecedented proportion, made me search more earnestly—inside myself, where I only came up empty, and then outside of myself, where others around me appeared to have an answer. The window of opportunity to be reached was opened a crack before I ever came to St. John's, but as my freshman year rolled along that window opened wider than the Granada without air conditioning along the hot Kansas highway. The road to find out led to St. John's College, and the experience at St. John's College led me to an encounter with Jesus. "What's the buzz, tell me what's a happening." I wanted to know—him.

"All we like sheep face the slaughter," I read in Romans 8. Now here was a Bible passage that described the St. John's Eagles basketball team. Perhaps sheep facing slaughter would have been a far more accurate if not so intimidating a mascot for us. Not that our opponents ever shook in their high-top sneakers when we showed up. We got slaughtered, not just once like a poor sheep, which would have been more merciful. We were slaughtered many times, over and over again, every single game. Losing so often by such margins took its toll, and basketball definitely lost its allure. The game that I loved so passionately was no longer lovable in the least, and playing was certainly not much fun anymore. Enrolling in St. John's in August and giving basketball a try had a reasonable, although slightly delusional, explanation. I had been extended an athletic scholarship and offered an opportunity to play college basketball. By contrast, returning to campus in January one week after withdrawing from school, quitting the team, packing up my belongings, and going home defied anything close to rationality. Miracles also defy reason, and I believed my return to Winfield to soldier onward was at least providential if not miraculous. Despite a repeated thumping game after miserable game, and even though my brother drove all the way to Kansas to pick me up, I had come too far to go back home and stay there. Billie analyzed that my experience had been valuable even if I decided to quit school:

> No matter what you think this semester has been good for you in many ways—not for basketball, but just learning to take care of yourself away from home—your joining the church—meeting people from places who you will probably never want to meet again, but just in passing by you have gained something from it.

By January, however, I sensed that there was more I was supposed to learn and more that I could expect to gain. Finally, I was ready. Getting baptized and joining the church were steps in the right direction, but a few more poundings on the basketball court proved necessary before it finally was pounded into my head, before it finally penetrated my heart. "All we like sheep face the slaughter," wrote St. Paul. Yes, slaughter I understood. "Yet, in all these things," Paul continued, "we are more than conquerors through him who loved us." Here was a compelling message for one who had grown so accustomed to tasting defeat. While undoubtedly I had been exposed to the general concept once or twice before—I may have even nailed questions correctly on a quiz in world's great religions—I finally understood the personal implication of what this meant for me. Along with understanding, at some indeterminate moment during my freshman year, I also believed. St. Paul punctuated his point with an exclamation: "For I am convinced that neither death nor life; neither angels nor demons; neither the present nor the future; nor any powers; nor height nor depth; nor anything else in all creation can separate us from the love of God in Christ Jesus our Lord." To his list I might have added neither homesickness nor loneliness, neither unfulfilled expectations nor broken dreams, neither losing nor even losing by a lot can separate us from God's love in Jesus. In fact, only through losing and facing slaughter could I really appreciate what it meant and how much it means to be "more than a conqueror." Offered a taste of something incomparably sweet, I slowly sipped before I drank more deeply. As promised, I was convinced as I tasted for myself that the Lord was good. Now I thirsted for even more.

There was no turning back, although by the end of my freshman year I perceived that I was drawing perilously close to becoming a dreaded "Jesus freak." Too close, in fact, to risk going home for the summer and facing the family and friends whom I had yearned to be near for most of the year. I still worried what others might think. That, coupled with my reluctance to return to the asphalt paving business, motivated me to ponder other possibilities. As Johnnies packed their bags to head for home, I left Winfield for Minneapolis at the invitation of my brother, Bob, to spend the summer with him, his wife, and their four-year-old daughter.

The four of us and a baby on the way—my sister-in-law was eight months pregnant—crowded into a little house that would have accommodated two people uncomfortably. I got a part-time job in an all-night grocery store and spent my days checking out the attractions of the Twin Cities with my brother. Once, on a trip to the bookstore on the campus of the University of Minnesota, where Bob was a doctoral student, I saw a biography of Martin Luther by Roland Bainton entitled *Here I Stand*. With one year at a Lutheran college behind me and another yet ahead, I impulsively surmised that knowing more about Martin Luther himself might serve me in good stead. It couldn't hurt. Ever short on cash, I got Bob to buy a copy of the paperback version for me. Whatever

I lacked in money was made up for in plenty of available time, so I began to read. Not since *Siddhartha* had I been so enthralled.

Martin Luther, I discovered early on in his biography, was also a man searching for answers. His quest for understanding was different from Siddhartha's circuitous path toward enlightenment. Luther was intimately familiar with suffering born of spiritual uncertainty, what the medieval mystics called "the long dark night of the soul." His own long dark night brought Luther little rest or peace—rest for his soul, or peace with God. Finally, looking to Christ alone for relief changed everything. Fear was replaced by faith, and despair gave way to hope.

In Psalm 30, King David's words also described Luther's experience, and to some extent mine: "I will exalt you, O Lord, for you lifted me out of the depths." The depths of darkness brought no little pain and anguish, but the Psalmist looked beyond the struggle, "Weeping may endure for a night, but joy comes in the morning." Always darkest before the dawn, it was now dawn nonetheless. At last the beginning of a brand new day and the long, dark midnight hour was over. Not that the road ahead would be swept from hardship or heartache, but at least there was now a clearer sense of direction and light for the way. The Psalmist also said, "You turned my wailing into dancing." Maybe Pogo's and Trinity had even more in common than I realized. He probably didn't know any disco moves, but in examining Luther's journey from deep darkness of doubt and gloom to marvelous light through confident faith in Jesus, I retraced a few of the steps that I had recently taken myself. Since Luther had been through it all and so much more before, I reckoned his experiences and insights could be useful to me as I went forward. A year of attending a Lutheran college, and also reading Bainton's book about Martin Luther, made me want to become a Lutheran myself. I guess I really was never much of a Methodist anyway.

The original plan to stay in Minnesota all summer was modified and abbreviated to six weeks. Leaving behind shelves that I stocked at the grocery store, I went back to Colorado, where my brother, Bill, pulled strings to get me back onto a paving crew for the next six weeks; back to Denver, where, a little sheepishly but unafraid of slaughter, I reconnected with my friends and family; and back home, where I asked the Petersons to make an appointment for me with the pastor at their church to see about becoming a member of the congregation. Pastor Zehnder, who grew up in Winfield, where his own father was once pastor at Trinity, assured me that I could complete the necessary instruction in the month and a half before school resumed. By the time I returned to St. John's College, I intended to be a Lutheran like the rest of the Johnnies. I could not wait to get back to Kansas.

I called Reed to let him know. He might as well be the first to be informed of the news. True to form, our pattern of not discussing religion during our Jefferson days had remained unchanged throughout our freshman year. Whatever I was experiencing, I kept it quiet and to myself. Reed, in particular, might expose my secrets to the folks back home if I wasn't careful. Now that I was back in town it didn't matter anymore. People were going to find out soon enough that I was a "Jesus freak" and in a few weeks would be a Lutheran one at that. I phoned him and told him that I was about to go through the required instruction at Bethlehem to become a member. Reed replied saying he was already a couple of weeks along the way in his own membership course at another nearby Lutheran church. Pastor John Rolf, Laura's father, who had sat across from us in the Campus Center at the banquet to welcome new freshmen, was his mentor. Now it was me who was blown away.

My alarm went off Monday morning while it was still dark outside, and I got up with the birds to report for work by the time bright finally caught up with early. It would be the first of lots of long summer days working on the streets and highways that other people would travel. As I grabbed the lunch Billie had packed for me and headed out the door, I felt excited about whatever direction the road ahead of me would lead. Backing out the driveway, I plugged an eight-track cassette into the tape deck. The rising sun signaled the night was past and heralded the dawn of a new day. I played Cat Stevens song about God's new creation and sang along. Now I had a sense of being part of that new creation myself:

Morning has broken, like the first morning.
Blackbird has spoken, like the first bird.

Praise for the singing, praise for the morning,
praise for the springing fresh from the world ... .

Praise with elation, praise every morning,
God's re-creation of the new day.

"MIDNIGHT TRAIN"
CHAPTER 8

June 2007–March 2008—"Midnight Train to Georgia" was Gladys Knight and the Pips' signature song. "L.A. was too much for the man." He was a "superstar who didn't get far." Now he was going back to the life he once knew on that midnight train to Georgia. Gladys Knight, meanwhile, was riding that train on her way to a Grammy Award in 1974.

The same summer Lefty and Billie took my sister and me on the two-day Amtrak train trip from Denver to Boston, where our New Hampshire relatives met us at the depot and drove us up the coast to their place. That excursion still ranks near the top of my all-time favorite travel experiences, and several times over the years I have checked into using Amtrak for my own family's summer vacation transport. One way to avert the monotony of all too familiar highway miles would be to travel by rail. Unfortunately, either inconvenience of itinerary or expense of fare repeatedly had kept me from springing for tickets. Finally this time I coordinated my calendar and put my money down months in advance of our family's June 2008 trip to Colorado to attend a wedding. In April we were all on board with the idea of an all-night train ride from Milwaukee to Denver.

The best laid plans, however, did not account for late spring floods in the Midwest that made rail lines impassable. Fortunately Amtrak provided a full refund, which I could use to pay for gasoline on the highway, meals at fast food joints located just off the exit ramps, and a night's stay somewhere in Nebraska at a hotel along the interstate. Without any other affordable alternative, we were set to get ourselves back on the road again.

With the change in plan, however, Andrew was more than happy to give up his seat in the family van and skip the trip. The floods were interpreted by him as a sign from God that he was not meant to travel west with the rest of us. Submerged rail lines in Iowa meant the only obstacle interfering with his quickly developing desire to get to Indiana for the summer school session was removed.

Earlier in the month Andrew and Tammy went to Valparaiso for freshman orientation and to register for fall semester classes. Before they left home I suggested that he contact Coach Drew to let him know that he was coming to campus. Homer invited Andrew to an open gym the evening before orientation if he happened to be in town. Although Andrew was clearly an afterthought and not on their radar—there had been virtually no communication from the coaching staff since indicating that he was going to attend Valpo—we were prepared to move heaven and earth to be sure that he was there for the unofficial practice. Nothing so strenuous was required. Andrew and his mom left Milwaukee a day early and checked into the Super 8.

Bryce Drew, Homer's son and top assistant, did a double take and told Andrew that he didn't recognize him when he came into the gym—the long-awaited growth spurt had finally commenced. Andrew now approached 6'2", as long as he kept his shoes on, and weighed nearly 170 pounds on a full stomach. His performance in the open gym also caught enough of the coaches' attention for them to mention the summer school option as a way to get a jump on workouts and get acquainted with the other freshmen. Homer noted that Andrew's game had come a long way since the only other time that he had seen him play—also at an open gym session in the spring. The coach also challenged Andrew to be a spiritual leader on the team and a positive influence for other incoming freshmen such as D'Andre Haskins, Erik Buggs, and Logan Jones. Bryce inquired whether Andrew had a preference for a number on his practice jersey, and urged him to keep working, lifting, eating, and taking protein. They promised to help find him one of the other basketball players for a roommate and said they would follow up in a few days about summer school.

Euphoric following the meeting, Andrew could hardly contain his enthusiasm. This all sounded like the first step toward his dream's coming true, and getting started immediately was not soon enough. Progress was measured in inches—the few he'd grown, and the ones that moved him within the coaches' line of sight. He still had far to go, but at least Homer wasn't raising the idea of Andrew as team manager any more. Skipping the family vacation was a small price to pay, not only in comparison to summer school tuition, but also for a chance to begin to prove his mettle. Maybe he wasn't a superstar, and maybe he wouldn't get far, but his train was about to leave the station and Andrew was sure he was on the right track. More accurately he was actually traveling back to Valpo for the summer session by automobile. Andrew loaded his mom's Toyota by himself and made the trek through Chicago to northwest Indiana solo.

Our middle son's departure for college came suddenly and two months sooner than the date for which we had been readying ourselves. Tammy and I weren't fully braced for the impact that comes when you let go, and on that day in June we were not even around to wave good-bye. I didn't lift a finger to pack his stuff in the car, or grab hold of the wheel to drive him safely through Chicago's traffic, or lend a hand to help him to unload. Nevertheless, my mind was on Andrew as we drove toward Denver, and I pondered what was going on in his mind as the first day of summer coincided with Andrew's first day of summer school:

> At the summer solstice of his life, Andrew chases his dreams and begins his flight of fancy. I have been living vicariously through his ascent for a long time and have enjoyed most of the ride. Now he's getting ready to leave the nest just like the little robins just outside our door did last week. About all I can do is hope that he lands on his feet—but before he does that I hope he soars farther than his dreams have imagined.

Before he could lift off, however, Andrew was well aware that he had to walk on.

He dresses up and wears the team uniform, but a "walk-on" is another way of describing a delusion masquerading as a dream. When he described to us the limited role of walk-ons during his long tenure as a college coach, Homer Drew practically gloated that only one player in nearly two decades had gone from being a walk-on to a scholarship player. He seemed almost proud of the fact. The quixotic quest of the walk-on was by no means limited to Valparaiso University. For every walk-on who eventually has an impact on a Division I basketball team, or who even gets a few meaningful minutes in a Division I basketball game, there are scores more who never score. In blowouts where the outcome of a contest is no longer contested a coach may occasionally point to the kid at the end of the bench. The walk-on frenetically rushes to the scorer's table and rips off his warm-ups in a single motion in order to forestall the resumption of action before he checks into the game. The crowd, or whatever remains of it after the rest have already headed for the exits, loves the underdog and cheers his appearance. They hope he manages to take a shot during his thirty-second stint on the floor; if the ball glances off the rim, the fans groan, but if somehow he miraculously drops one through the net they erupt. The buzzer sounds, and people grab their coats and make a beeline for the parking lot. The walk-on retrieves his warm-ups and heads for the locker room and a hot shower. His uniform is thrown in a pile to be laundered with the rest. The walk-on's dreams, meanwhile, get a rude awakening with a cold splash of reality.

In the sweaty summer months before his freshman season, the idea of a cold splash of anything, including reality, did not concern Andrew. He was welcomed on to the basketball team at Division I Valparaiso University, and given enough time and opportunity he would earn his keep. Valparaiso's is a big enough program in a small enough town that almost no basketball news goes unnoticed. During the summertime even walk-ons get some attention. In early July the local *Post-Tribune* ran an article about Andrew's roommate, D'Andre Haskins, an athletic guard who was from California but who attended high school in nearby LaPorte, Indiana. Andrew garnered a few lines in the piece as well:

> Andrew Ferry, a point guard out of Milwaukee Lutheran High School will be a walk-on for Valparaiso this year. Ferry averaged 18.5 points and hit a school record 74 3-pointers in 22 games last year.
>
> Ferry's been on campus the last couple of weeks working out with several players, including Logan Jones and Haskins. "We've been working out daily," Ferry said. "They're good workouts—tough but fun."
>
> Homer Drew said Ferry will fill a valuable role for VU. "He's a wonderful Valpo kid—an 'A' student, so he'll fit in academically, and a really good shooter, so he'll fit in basketball-wise," Drew said.

The more that Mark Lazerus, the sportswriter for the *Post-Tribune,* thought it over, the more he felt should be said about the freshman walk-on's impending prospects. Besides, in July there was not much else to write about related to Crusader hoops. The day after he introduced Andrew as a new player on Valpo's team, Lazerus wrote a column on the front page of the sports section entitled "VU walk-on Ferry takes on a thankless role." Lazerus offered his assessment of exactly what Andrew faced:

> Here's what Andrew Ferry has to look forward to this year—and potentially the three years that follow. Long, grueling practices. Endless weight-lifting sessions and diet restrictions. Countless hours on a bus. Curfews, a cramped social life, lost weekends. And a $30,000 bill to pay.
>
> "It's just kind of my dream," he said.

Ah, the life of a walk-on. This is the path Ferry—a 6 foot, 155-pound guard out of Milwaukee—chose when he took Homer Drew up on his invitation to be a walk-on at Valparaiso.

Ferry, a 3-point specialist who set school records from beyond the arc and averaged more than 18 points per game as a senior, had offers from Division II and Division III schools—but he wanted to play Division I basketball. Always has. And his only option was to pay his own way, and hopefully earn his way into a scholarship.

"I think I can do it," Ferry said. "I wouldn't have come if I didn't think I could. I think I'm a really hard-working person and I like challenges. I'm up to it."

But Ferry's no dummy—you can't get into a school such as VU if you are, especially when you're just a regular run-of-the-mill student, not a high-profile student-athlete on scholarship. He knows the odds are incredibly stacked against him. Not everyone—in fact, hardly anyone—can pull off what Dwayne Toatley did eight years ago and earn a scholarship in the middle of his college career.

And Drew, while he didn't outright puncture Ferry's dream made sure the freshman realized this fact. "He was more realistic about it," Ferry said. "He told me it would be tough, and that he hasn't had too many guys who had been successful with it. He didn't want to discourage me, but he kept it real ... ."

Maybe sometime down the road, Ferry will face the difficult decision (to transfer). But for now, he's ecstatic to be at VU—he first visited as a seventh-grader in a national Lutheran grade school tournament—and playing whatever role he's asked.

And it is a big role. An important role. Just not a high-profile role. And not a very cost-effective one either. For now, though, Ferry's fine with all that. He knows his role. "My job right now is to help every day and push people to get better," he said. "This year's not going to be my year, and maybe next year won't, either. But, my goal is to contribute."

He will. The only question is how.

At Valpo Andrew would have to compete with more highly recruited and very athletic kids. Overcoming whatever advantages other players may have had over him was not going to be easy. Surmounting the coach's modest expectations might be even tougher. In order to convince Homer Drew that he deserved a shot he would have to really stand out. "My guess is that Andrew is in just the right spot for a more compelling story." In my journal I observed that this had all the right ingredients for one of those moving tales of overcoming all odds and achieving success. Of course, there remained the not-so-small matter of actually realizing success. If the walk-on in the article in the Valpo paper was to have a glowing tribute at the end of his career as a Crusader there was still much ground to cover. "Stories like that just don't happen very often," I acknowledged. "Every kid (and his Dad) who walks-on imagines that he will be the long shot who comes through." Andrew's advantage, to be sure, was that long shots were his forte—as a player and as a person. "Few shoot as well as he does. Few have to overcome the physical challenges he has faced, from late growth spurt to diabetes." While not much of a gambler, I wrote "given Andrew's work ethic and determination, I wouldn't bet against him."

Others, including his coaches, were skeptical about Andrew's odds of making much of a difference at Valpo. "He needs me to believe in him," I wrote in my journal. "I do." But, even if I didn't, and even if I joined the ranks of those who don't expect him to achieve much in basketball at Valpo, I knew that Andrew would be undeterred. He embraced the nay-saying as added opportunity to prove something to everybody. "Andrew is ready to take on the world and nothing—not diabetes, not lack of height nor weight nor speed nor strength, not any coach's minimal expectation—will dissuade him. He won't go down without a fight." Whether Andrew benefited earlier from my help to get his foot in the door was no longer consequential. "My entreaties have only allowed a tiny window of opportunity. All he needs is a crack. Andrew will take care of the rest." If things never panned out, what difference did it make? "Andrew can't lose," I reasoned. "Whatever he achieves at Valpo will be beyond anybody's expectation." Except maybe mine, and certainly his own.

I believed in Andrew, but I believed in God more. Trusting that the Lord would not lead my son down any blind alleys, I had faith that Andrew's ending up at Valpo was part of a divine design and plan for his life. My own freshman year I derived consolation from the Romans 8 passage in which St. Paul says that in Christ we are "more than conquerors" despite all the trials and troubles that assail us. Now that Andrew approached his own first year, another verse from the same Romans 8 chapter spoke to me. As Andrew took his turn at being a freshman and playing college basketball on a much bigger stage, I was buoyed by St. Paul's words that "All things work together for good for those who love God and who are called according to his purpose."

No matter what transpired in the coming year, I grabbed hold of the promise that this experience would be good for Andrew, and good in a way that was in accord with God's own definition. *"Andrew's story* will be a good one," I predicted, "if he grasps the spiritual dimension." One of the reasons I wanted him to attend Wheaton College was because I knew he could not avoid the question of where he fit into God's plan—not where God fit into Andrew's plan. "Valpo should also give him a chance to figure that out, and Coach Homer Drew is certainly mindful of bigger meanings in life that transcend basketball." Until the outcome became clearer, with pen and journal in hand, I said, "I'll keep writing, and I'll keep praying, and I'll keep encouraging, and I'll keep trying to interpret what it all might mean."

By summer's end Andrew had begun to make a favorable first impression on his coaches. He called to report that Bryce took him to the side after one workout and told him he was probably the best shooter on the team. The challenge would be to translate his effectiveness in drills into shots taken in games, but Andrew felt he had competed well all summer. Homer wrote us a complimentary note, "You raised a wonderful son … his work ethic is awesome!!" The coach also phoned us to discuss the management of Andrew's diabetes and wanted to be sure that we were all on the same page. We assured him that we were confident that Andrew was very capable of effectively caring for himself because he was a disciplined kid. Homer affirmed Andrew's self-discipline as well as his dedication. "The team would have no problems," he said, "if only they were all like Andrew." Coach Drew took Andrew's daily diabetic struggle personally. He organized his players and had them participate in a walk to raise awareness and funds for the Juvenile Diabetes Research Foundation, and Andrew was touched by the show of support and solidarity from his teammates and coaches. There was no doubt in Andrew's mind that this place was exactly where he was supposed to be.

The athletic department featured Andrew in the fall issue of a newsletter that it sends to young Crusader fans. Next to his picture in a Valpo uniform ran the headline: "Living with Diabetes: Freshman Andrew Ferry." The story described Andrew's diagnosis during his sophomore year in high school and went on to say:

> Now Andrew is starting his freshman year at Valpo, and he is proof that people with diabetes can do whatever they set their minds to .... Andrew hasn't let diabetes stop him from becoming a great basketball player, and earning a spot on this year's Valpo team.

A writer for another local daily newspaper, the *Northwest Indiana Times*, got to know Andrew and also became familiar with the diabetes story. David Robb penned a column in early October entitled "Ferry the Crusader keeps up the fight":

> At first Andrew Ferry thought it was just a cold. And then his tongue turned white, his muscles cramped up and his thirst became unquenchable.

> As a walk-on freshman with the Valparaiso University men's basketball team, Ferry isn't just fighting for playing time. He's constantly fighting a disease that affects 23.6 million Americans, or nearly 8% of the population.

> Ferry was diagnosed with Type 1 diabetes at 16. The bad news came smack dab in the middle of the basketball season—January 1, 2006. But Ferry, then a sophomore at Milwaukee Lutheran, didn't fret. He didn't pout. And he certainly didn't quit. He suited up—a day after being diagnosed ....

> And here he is at VU, after turning down several Division II offers,

preparing to take the next step in a career that even diabetes could not derail.

"I don't think I feel sorry for myself," Ferry said. "I've tried to embrace it and tried to use it to my advantage. I think that's all you can do, try to help other people with it, be kind of a role model for others. You can't let it bring you down."

Ferry never does. He and his new VU teammates and coaching staff participated in the Walk to Cure Diabetes last Sunday at Hidden Lake Park in Merrillville. The event helped raise money for the Juvenile Diabetes Research Foundation.

The walk was nothing new for Ferry, who was a youth ambassador for the American Diabetes Association in high school and even filmed a commercial with a Milwaukee Brewers broadcaster to promote a fundraising event.

"When I first learned about it, I realized it was serious," Ferry said of his diagnosis. "I realized how it was going to shape the rest of my life."

In high school Ferry gave himself shots to control his blood sugar. Last March he switched to a wireless pump, which is programmed to feed him insulin throughout the day.

In order to make the switch, Ferry had to chart what he ate and how much insulin he gave himself for two weeks. But, the real burden was having to wake himself up every two hours to check his blood sugar. "That was not a fun two weeks," Ferry said.

Even with the wireless pump, which he wears on his stomach at all times—even while playing—Ferry still has to prick his finger

10-15 times daily to check his blood sugar, still has to count his carbohydrates every meal, still has to be more responsible than your average college freshman.

"I wouldn't say it makes basketball more difficult," Ferry said. "It just means you have to be more alert to whatever is going on with your body and to be more disciplined."

And more determined.

Already for a second time Andrew was featured in a front-page story in one of Valparaiso's daily newspapers, and the basketball season had yet to officially start. Between them, sportswriters Mark Lazerus and David Robb articulated the double-decker dilemma Andrew faced in trying to reach his goal and play Division I basketball. Not only was he a walk-on, but Andrew was a walk-on engaged in a daily fight with a disease that required constant vigilance to stay alive. He was an undersized guard going up against twin towers anchored in the center of the lane, blocking his way and cutting off his penetration.

Had they merely been other basketball players, scooting around them would have been easier. Adept enough after a year and a half of experience at getting past the diabetes difficulties, no mere life-threatening disease by itself would bring Andrew down. The limitations attached to being a lowly walk-on, on the other hand, loomed larger. His usual tactics of outworking and outshooting everybody else brought no promise of playing time. Even comments like "Andrew is the best walk-on we've ever had," did not guarantee moving upward in the pecking order off the end of the bench. The distance from where Andrew would sit in a cushioned chair as a reserve on the sideline to the place he might let loose a deep three-point shot from the corner was only a foot or two at most. Yet, the chasm created by the out-of-bounds line was almost impossible to bridge. Once the season officially began Andrew learned that a walk-on, and a freshman walk-on in particular, would bump up against his limits pretty quickly.

In the team's preseason closed scrimmage at Northwestern University Andrew played sparingly. The opening exhibition game at home against Division III Elmhurst was a runaway trounce for Valpo, but Andrew did not enter the game until the final few minutes. Andrew was disappointed and a little shocked, even though this was essentially the scenario described by Homer Drew in advance. In practice he felt that he was competing well. The coaches occasionally singled out his effort and encouraged him to keep working hard. This was no time to feel sorry for himself. His chance would come, he felt sure, so Andrew kept plugging away. The pattern, however, remained unchanged.

Valpo was mired in an early season slump. The commentators on the Webcasts repeatedly lamented the team's lack of a consistent outside shooting threat. Tammy and I squirmed as we watched, our only glimpses of Andrew during timeouts when he rushed to greet his teammates huddling around the coach for instructions. We reminded ourselves that Andrew was just a freshman and not to become impatient. But, there were four other freshman scholarship players that played plenty. The roster was depleted when two returning players defected after the previous year and another suffered a knee injury. Younger guys were being thrown into the fray—except for the walk-on, who bided his time. Always more content to delay gratification than I was, Andrew gave no clues of being disappointed about seldom seeing action. The team's losses mounted, but Andrew kept his composure. Once in a while I lost mine, but I constantly tried visualizing ways in which "all things were working together for good" and comparing Andrew's unfolding saga to my own freshman season three decades before:

> My past I can recount and put into order. Andrew's story continues to play out. I pray about Andrew's freshman year. It does not resemble mine, but it preoccupies me nearly as much now as mine did then.
>
> I fret about what to think, what to counsel, what to want, what to pray. Of course, I want Andrew to gain whatever the Lord wants him to learn and grow from his time there. But, I also want to offer lots of ideas about what I think would be best and supply my own storylines as suggestions for the Lord's consideration. My plot includes lots of playing time and Andrew having considerable success as a player, as a student, as a young man—as a young man of God.
>
> I'd have Andrew gathering enough basketball glory to give him a platform to glorify God. I'd have Andrew gaining enough notoriety to draw attention to the fight against Type 1 diabetes. If I could write the script I'd have Andrew overcoming the obstacles he's already faced, those he now encounters, and others still ahead with an almost made-for-motion pictures story. Too bad I can't write the script ahead of time.
>
> Right now it doesn't look like all that much of a story. It might be next to impossible for Andrew to get off the bench this season, or next, or ever. He might get frustrated and lose interest. Even if he perseveres and pushes harder there is no promise that it will pay off as he might hope.

I do trust that Andrew, to the extent that he bothers to reflect on his own freshman year and college basketball, will see God's hand in it all clearly enough. For the moment it is not that obvious. I guess that is what faith is about.

There were some intriguing twists in the tale even as Andrew waited patiently, and I waited impatiently, for the Lord and Coach Drew to help make the plot thicken. A few days before Christmas Valparaiso hosted the North Carolina Tar Heels in Chicago at the United Center, the home of the NBA Chicago Bulls. For as long as I could remember I had been a loyal North Carolina fan, and for the first time I was about to see them play in person—against my son's team! Whatever the struggles of the season to date, this was a special occasion. The day before the game I looked forward to the moment and measured its meaning in my journal:

> Wouldn't it be ironic, though, if Andrew began to get his big break against North Carolina? That would be something not only because they are the number one team in the country, but also (and especially for me) because they have long been the number one team in my heart. I am writing the book, but I don't get to make up the story. Fairy Tales and Ferry Tales are not the same thing. Once in awhile the truth is stranger than fiction. More often, however, the truth is pretty boring.

Through the years I have been able to see the humor and appreciate the significance of my freshman year of basketball. I suspect the same thing will one day be true for Andrew. Already he is learning painful lessons that come from losing, learning about patience, about budgeting time, about delayed (if ever) gratification, about lots of stuff.

Making some big shots against the top team in the country is part of the fantasy of long hours shooting in the driveway. In real life you probably don't even get on to the floor. The magical Fairy Tale ends with a game-winning three-point shot at the buzzer. The mundane Ferry Tale is finding satisfaction in watching your son get to warm up in the arena where Michael Jordan, North Carolina's most famous player, became the best player on the planet. It comes in just being satisfied that your kid as a college freshman gets to warm up before the game against your childhood favorite, and maybe even get a few minutes of playing time before the final buzzer sounds—maybe.

No, real life is not as fantastic as fantasy, but it is not so bad. At least it doesn't have to be.

Valpo ignored reality and played North Carolina even for the first ten minutes. At the break the Tar Heels led 41–31, but the Crusaders certainly had overachieved their way into a respectable showing. The best team in the country systematically wore down Valpo and extended the margin in the second half. Late in the game the benches for both teams were cleared. Andrew checked in, and we watched intently. Some of his friends watched on TV. Afterward I wrote:

> Someday, many years from now, the only thing that will matter about today's game against North Carolina is that Andrew got to play, and he scored. In his brief two minutes at the end he had a three-point shot rim out, and missed the first of two free throws but made the second. He also got a rebound and a steal. It was not

near long enough, but most of our memories are condensed into a little, tiny thought—a sound bite and mental image that can be described in a few words.

Andrew will remember today. So will I. He played against the top-ranked Tar Heels. So what if Valpo lost 85–62? So what if he got in long after the outcome was settled? Today he got to do something that most boys who play basketball only dream about. Andrew got to play—and score—against North Carolina.

In early January Andrew made a trip home for Valpo's game against the University of Wisconsin–Milwaukee. My own expectations for his much anticipated homecoming game were pretty low. The team continued its downward spiral, and Andrew could only watch. Once the game got out of reach, assuming Milwaukee would eventually pull away, I hoped that Homer might insert Andrew for some token time. There would likely be a good showing of support for Andrew from family and friends. His Milwaukee Lutheran coaches switched around practice schedules to allow the kids and themselves to get downtown to watch. When Andrew appeared in the final few minutes he drew applause from all corners of the US Cellular Arena, the UWM Panthers' home court. Once the raucous student section of UWM figured out that Andrew had many partisans in the crowd, they joined to cheer each of the few times he touched the ball and grimaced in mock agony when his desperate shots failed to go down. Well-wishers lined up after the game to pat Andrew on the back and encourage him. "Hang in there," they told him. My strong suspicion was this might be his first, last, and only chance to play for Valpo in his hometown.

I did some soul-searching after the UWM game and lamented

the role that I had played in Andrew's planning and preparation the previous few years and concluded:

> I failed to give him an adequate sense of reality. He should have heard from me that he was not capable of playing at a place like Valpo, and the skills that he does have would be far better put to use at a different level. He has had a dream that I have helped to perpetuate rather than helping him to approach all of this realistically.

> On the other hand, is it not my job to encourage him to chase his dreams rather than restrain him with the ropes of reality? Why tie him down without at least giving him a chance to fly? The failure to reach his goals is not a sin. Perhaps the greater wrong would be not to try. There is no doubt he is trying and trying very hard. There is plenty of doubt, at least on my part, that he will be successful or even get a real chance to succeed.

In middle January, the week after the loss at Milwaukee, Homer faced further bad news. More injuries, including a concussion suffered by starting guard Erik Buggs, left him with only six scholarship players in uniform. Suddenly Andrew was the seventh man. All week he practiced in expectation of playing what he called "legit" minutes against Loyola University in Chicago. The coaches prepared him for a role in the game plan, and Andrew was excited and ready to go. By most measures Andrew had played a fair amount already for a freshman, especially for a walk-on. Homer had probably given him more time than anyone, including the coach, imagined. My frustration was that the circumstances should have made even more opportunity available. Now Homer had little choice, and Andrew was poised to take advantage of the situation.

Loyola beat Valpo 71–56, and Andrew played a grand total of 32 seconds in the first half and 11 seconds in the second half. I had stayed home to attend my youngest son, Stephen's, junior varsity game, but Tammy traveled to Loyola. I recorded my impressions of Andrew's reactions based on her conversation with him following the game:

> He felt insulted, I think. Tammy was in tears describing how he tried to be positive and upbeat, but he was deeply hurt. All of the preparation, and all the indications that he would get his chance never happened. If they didn't occur in that setting and situation they never will. Andrew, fortunately, now recognizes that is true. He also recognizes that it is time to move on.
>
> That is hard for him. First, because he likes Valpo—the school, the team, the coaches. Second, because he is convinced that he is capable of playing well at that level. But, he is able to sort it out enough to realize that he won't ever really get the chance to play in meaningful moments of the game. Walk-ons just don't fit the plan.
>
> He called to talk to me about it last night. Of course, he will finish out the year and take as much from the experience as he possibly can. I have urged him to take the high road—to be positive and work hard. Andrew doesn't need that advice from me. That's how he is.

The game at Loyola was the low point of the season for Andrew and for his parents. His chance to play would evaporate as injured players resurfaced in the lineup, and Andrew returned to his customary position deeper down the depth chart. If he wasn't going to see action when only seven guys were suited, his likelihood of setting foot on the floor as the ninth or tenth man was only further diminished. Up until now he'd patiently maintained an upbeat attitude. Even if this year he saw only limited playing time, eventually his day would come. The decimation of the roster due to injuries, he believed, accelerated the process, and the future was now. If that was so, the future was much different from what he had hoped.

As he sat on the bench near enough to the coaches to hear them breathe and almost close enough to hear them think, Andrew sighed as he came face to face with the implications of the Loyola game for his career at Valpo. As his teammates crashed to yet another disappointing loss, the vision of the road ahead showed signs of an imminent and sharp detour. He obviously did not fit into Homer's scheme at all for this year, and with a slew of recruits already signed and sealed for next season, he saw little possibility of ever having an impact in a Valpo uniform. When the team returned home from Chicago, Andrew, as was his custom, grabbed a ball and worked out on his own. He dropped forty consecutive three-point shots by a teammate's count. Andrew wasn't keeping track. As far as he was concerned the only long-shot attempt that mattered had missed, and the detour required him to concentrate on his exit strategy.

Of course, the Crusaders had plenty of troubles without worrying about the disappointment of a walk-on freshman. When the season commenced Homer Drew needed a mere seven wins to reach the lofty plateau of six hundred career coaching victories. Only a handful of collegiate coaches preceded him to that accomplishment, and initially it was considered by most fans to be only a matter of time, even in a rebuilding year, before the milestone was achieved. Coach Drew indicated that six hundred was merely a number and was far less concerned than others, perhaps including the university's public relations department, about the significance of the achievement. As Valpo's season began to tank, however, questions began to be raised about whether this year's team would reach the requisite but elusive seven victories. They were stuck on six and going nowhere fast.

Time was running out, but, fortunately, the February 7th game at Detroit was on the horizon of the Horizon League schedule. Detroit's Titans were in last place, and a month earlier at home in Valparaiso the Crusaders, dispatched them with relative ease, 64–41. By all accounts the remainder of the schedule looked much stiffer, and there was a distinct possibility that given Valpo's struggles Detroit might well represent the last, best hope for the team to deliver number six hundred to coach Drew this year.

"Pathetic," was the word that Homer used to describe the 56–55 loss at Detroit, as Valpo squandered a late lead and a chance to win. This was a new low point for an already dismal season. The team's record dipped to 6–18, and, considering the string of uninspiring recent outings, securing even one more check in the victory column this year was questionable. Indeed, winning again now looked almost improbable. Andrew did not get into the Detroit game—since the score was so close that came as no surprise. But, because his departure from Valpo after his freshman year had become more or less a foregone conclusion, Andrew decided to speak to Homer now rather than wait until a postseason debriefing. There was nothing to lose by telling Coach Drew that he honestly believed that he could help the team with a legitimate chance to compete. Instead of his regular ritual of shooting jumpers in the gym after the bus dropped off the team back on campus, Andrew risked the ire of stirring a coach still fuming after a tough loss. He knocked on Homer's door.

According to Andrew, the conversation was very cordial. Even better, Homer said the coaches were in agreement that other guys were not getting the job done, and that Andrew deserved a chance. The next game was at home on Friday the 13th against Loyola. It was an inauspicious date to play against a team that brought Andrew heartache once already as he sat agonizingly on the bench waiting in futility for his number to be called. "Maybe this time," Andrew said hopefully. "I'll believe it when I see it," I muttered inaudibly to myself, "we've heard this all before."

Even if he did manage to touch the ball or just get a whiff of action, I wouldn't view it on the Web or listen on the radio. Instead I would be planted in the bleachers at Milwaukee Lutheran's gym rooting on my daughter, Rachel, who would be playing the last home game of her senior year on Parents' Night. My commitment from the outset of basketball season was to avoid being diverted from any of Rachel's games during her last year. In Milwaukee Lutheran's conference, boy's and girl's teams were scheduled on the same nights against the same opponents. However, they played the games in opposite gymnasiums. Thus, much to my frustration and consternation, I had missed many of her games during her junior year when Andrew was a senior. This year belonged to my daughter, and her final game at home was my particular priority. No way was I going to be distracted by the remote possibility of Andrew's getting a few minutes against Loyola when I knew Rachel would play plenty against Nicolet. I vowed to concentrate on her game only, although occasional thoughts about how things were going in Indiana managed to creep into my mind.

At halftime, however, I figured a quick peek at my BlackBerry to check the score was not in violation of the spirit of my intention. Surprisingly, Valpo led Loyola 33–19 at the intermission. Scrolling down further to the game's stats, I was flabbergasted to read that Andrew Ferry was 2–2 from the field and had five points! Was there really any harm in keeping tabs on Valpo and Loyola on the Blackberry while watching the rest of Rachel's game? I released myself from my vow for the second half.

Obviously, I could not be in two places at once to see and hear what was happening at the Valpo game, but I got a flavor afterward reading through the live blogs that had been posted every few minutes by Mark Lazerus at the *Post-Tribune* and by Paul Jankowski at the *Northwest Indiana Times*. Using this method to communicate with Valpo faithful anywhere and everywhere, these reporters provided their own running commentary for most home games. Their blogs replaced what would have been my own more biased analysis had I been in Valpo's bleachers instead of Milwaukee Lutheran's that night. I imagined myself looking over their shoulder as they watched or eavesdropping on their remarks as they assessed the game. What follows was their periodic impression.

Paul Jankowski reported first:

7:12 p.m.—The Crusaders are up 5–2 with 15:55 remaining and the game has been sloppy so far. Both teams have three turnovers already. In an interesting move, freshman walk-on Andrew Ferry is checking into the game for Buggs instead of Logan Jones. This is the time that Jones normally comes in and this is by far the earliest that Ferry has seen court time in a game. Hmmm.

7:18 p.m.—Good ball movement has helped the Crusaders open an 11–2 lead with 13:02 left in first half as Ferry and Howard Little have knocked down 3-pointers. Ferry's shot drew a huge reaction from the crowd as the walk-on is playing the most important minutes of his career right now.

7:21 p.m.—The Crusaders are playing with fire and determination reminiscent of their last victory which came against Milwaukee here at home on January 22nd. Ferry has given the team a boost … .

Mark Lazerus also took note:

7:21 p.m.–VU 15, Loyola 4, 11:32 left in first half: Well, lookee here. For some reason, Drew puts in Andrew Ferry ahead of Logan Jones after the first media timeout, and Ferry knocks down a wide-open 3-pointer to make it 8–2. When things are working, they're working.

Jankowski, a few minutes later:

7:36 p.m.—Ferry shows that he has range from inside the arc with a nice pull-up jumper that gives him a career high five points. The Crusaders are up 23–12 with just over five minutes in the first half.

Lazerus was next:

7:39 p.m.—VU 25, Loyola 15, 3:49 left in first half: Never mind all these guys coming in next year, give Andrew Ferry a scholarship! Back in with 6:17 to go, Ferry promptly faked a 3, dribbled forward and drilled a jumper for a career high five points. He's 2-of-2. He's been the highlight so far in what has been a very sloppy game … Still no Logan Jones sighting. He's on the bench, but not the court. Hmmm … .

In the second half Jankowski posted one more observation:

8:27 p.m.—Ferry has continued to shuffle in and out of the lineup and now has played a career-high ten minutes … .

A lot of love was shown to Homer Drew on Valentine's Day in the next morning's papers to celebrate his long-awaited six hundredth victory. The coach humbly deflected the accolades and credited his success to others. Valpo's 71–47 win over Loyola was easily the team's most impressive performance of the season. "Drew finally captures No. 600," read the headline at the top of the sports section of the *Times.* Much farther down in the article there was also this mention: "And even walk-on Andrew Ferry contributed, scoring a career-high seven points which included five in the first half." I wondered to myself how significant was the connection between Andrew's long-awaited debut and his role as a catalyst to the long-awaited six hundredth victory.

Valpo had little time to rest on Homer's well-deserved laurels. The University of Illinois–Chicago Flames came to town for a Sunday afternoon game, and both of the Sunday morning papers provided previews. Each also took note of Andrew's efforts on the previous Friday night. In the *Post-Tribune*, Mark Lazerus wrote:

Also, walk-on freshman Andrew Ferry bumped Logan Jones for the backup point guard spot, at least for the day. Jones was not injured and did play a little, but Ferry set a career high of seven points (2-of-2 from the field) in 11 minutes.

"Andrew's really been playing well," Drew said. "He's spent a lot of time working on his shot and ball-handling, and he just deserved the opportunity. He responded very well."

Meanwhile, the *Times* reporter, Paul Jankowski, devoted more ink to the story. Alongside a mug shot of Andrew, Jankowski wrote a full article under the heading, "Ferry comes through when it counts." Jankowski wrote:

> After every home game, Valparaiso freshman walk-on Andrew Ferry is always the last to leave the gym.
>
> Ferry is one of a handful of players who practice shooting on the Athletics-Recreation Center floor after the crowd has filed out. One could joke that it's the only time Ferry sees the court on game night, but that wasn't the case Friday.
>
> Head coach Homer Drew called Ferry's number early in the first half of a 71–54 victory over Loyola. Ferry entered the game at the 15:54 mark, replacing Eric Buggs in a spot of the rotation normally reserved for Logan Jones.
>
> Less than two minutes later, Ferry found himself wide open for a 3-pointer. He nailed it, nothing but net.
>
> "Andrew has really been playing well in practice, and he just deserved the opportunity to have that chance," Drew said. "He played very well and handled the ball well."
>
> Ferry added a jumper and two free throws for seven points while playing eleven minutes, both career highs. And most importantly, Ferry was on the floor when it counted and didn't miss a shot attempt.
>
> "It was a great feeling," Ferry said while taking a break from his post-game shooting routine. "I just wanted to reward my coaches' confidence and do what I can to help my team win."

That's nothing new for Ferry. At Milwaukee Lutheran High School he was MVP on a team that won two regional titles. Ferry set school records for three-pointers in a season (74) and in a game (eight) as a senior.

So Ferry's a shooter, but at a generously listed 6-foot-2 and 170 pounds, Division I scholarship offers didn't pour in. Ferry played in the annual National Lutheran Basketball Tournament at Valpo as a youngster, and wanted to play for the Crusaders.

"I try to work hard every day so when my chance does come, I'm able to come through," Ferry said. "You like to see the benefits of your work, and (against Loyola) I was able to see that. If the chance comes again, I'll be ready ... ."

He had to get ready quickly that Sunday afternoon because early in the UIC game Andrew was summoned to enter. Paul Jankowski blogged:

3:13 p.m.—With 15:50 remaining the Flames are up 8–4. Andrew Ferry has already checked into the game and the freshman walk-on is continuing to earn important minutes ahead of classmate Logan Jones. Is the message being sent to Jones? Is this the product of Ferry's hard work? Regardless, the freshman showed his hustle on his first possession as he dove for a loose ball and kept the play alive.

A few minutes later he added:

3:30 p.m.—Rogers, Ferry, and Witt are currently outscoring the Valparaiso starters 14–7 (and by starters I mean Igbvaboa and Diebler as Little, Haskins and Buggs have yet to find the basket).

Valpo led UIC 43–40 at intermission. Andrew played five intense minutes before exiting to an appreciative round of applause from the home crowd. During the second stanza Coach Drew left Andrew languishing on the bench once again, and the Crusaders let their lead slip en route to an 83–76 defeat. Of course, I noted that the loss of the lead coincided with Andrew's idleness and suspected connections that only a father might claim.

The following Saturday was another home tilt, the so-called ESPN "Bracket Buster" against the Akron Zips, the top team in the Mid-America Conference. Barring a miracle in the Horizon League conference tournament, Valpo was not in line for a postseason appearance, but at 17–9 the Zips certainly had genuine March Madness prospects. Andrew had been advised by Homer that he would not likely see much action against the quick, athletic Akron backcourt, and his repetitions in practice during the week shrank noticeably. The coach's strategy changed, however, when Akron took advantage of too many Valpo turnovers and jumped out to a big lead. Paul Jankowski described what came next:

> 7:31 p.m.—Drew takes a timeout simply to put Andrew Ferry in the game for Buggs. Akron is playing with the kind of aggression and reckless abandon that was displayed by many of the NCAA tournament teams Valpo has faced. Zips lead 31–17 with 7:43 remaining.

Maybe I still saw connections that were figments of my imagination, but soon after Andrew checked in and got into the flow, Jankowski blogged:

> 7:43 p.m.—The Crusaders respond with a 10–0 run ... and are within seven at 39–32 with 3:50 remaining in the first half.

The shift in momentum continued and Akron's lead began to erode. Describing action in the second half, Jankowski commented:

> 8:17—Valparaiso is staying in the game as Akron is up 51–45 with 15:58 remaining .... Buggs has not played in the second half and now Andrew Ferry is checking in the game. Not only has Ferry supplanted Logan Jones in the rotation, but now he's coming in the game in front of Buggs. Interesting.

> 9:10—Valparaiso 74, Akron 66. That's the win of the year folks.

Akron's bracket may not have been totally busted, but Valpo did some serious damage to the Zips' hopes of an at-large invitation to the NCAA tournament. Only a victory in the MAC conference tournament, with its automatic bid, would secure a spot in the field for Akron.

Our bloggers were also active during Valpo's game at home toward the end of the season against Cleveland State, another NCAA tournament hopeful. Paul Jankowsi was first to comment on Andrew as the Crusaders struggled to keep pace with the powerful Vikings:

> 8:08 p.m.—Andrew Ferry just checked into the game ... ahead of Logan Jones and ahead of Erik Buggs. I bet getting benched in favor of a walk-on wasn't in the brochure when Jones and Buggs decided to sign with Valparaiso last year.

Mark Lazerus noted Valparaiso's effectiveness midway through the first period:

> 8:15 p.m.—VU 15, CSU 11, 10:33 left in the first half: VU's looking good offensively, hitting 6-of-8 from the field .... All this with Jake Diebler and sometimes walk-on Andrew Ferry on the court.

The walk-on spent no time on the court a week later as the Valparaiso Crusaders were eliminated in the first round of the Horizon League tournament, falling to Wright State 68–56 in Dayton, Ohio. Coach Drew stayed with his regulars when faced with the ultimatum of "win or go home." Valpo went home and ended the season 9–22. I couldn't resist noting that following the Detroit debacle they were 3–3 down the stretch in the six games that Andrew played at least a few meaningful minutes. I suspect nobody else noticed but me.

An hour after the final game of his freshman year, I phoned Andrew to tell him that I was proud of him. His pluck and perseverance were an inspiration to me. As far as I was concerned, nobody deserved success more than he did. Andrew's dream was to play Division I basketball. "I proved that I can do it," he said to me. Indeed.

Already the next day back in Valparaiso the coaching staff called for one-on-one meetings with each player before sending the guys along their way for spring vacation. They were wonderfully affirming of Andrew as a person and as a player and invited him to continue to be part of the program. However, Homer also wanted to be honest and forthcoming. There were no scholarships available, and they were counting on their new recruits to step in and have immediate impact. Andrew, once again, would be relegated to the bottom rung of the ladder with limited opportunity to climb even as far as he had in recent weeks. Homer confessed that it brought him to tears to come to this conclusion, but he believed that Andrew deserved to play rather than sit and thus should probably pursue other options. Anything he could do to assist, Coach Drew promised to do. Homer graciously telephoned me to relate the same message. My son shed a few tears of his own, but he called to let me know that he got the word that he needed to hear. It wasn't the midnight train; Tammy picked him up in the Camry to bring him home for the break. Andrew was not a superstar, but he made it remarkably far—at least in my book. Now it was time to begin a new chapter.

EPILOGUE

Easter 2009—When Reed Lessing and I returned to St. John's College for our sophomore year, we were accompanied by two other friends from Jefferson—one a transfer student who had been in our class of 1977, the other a brand new freshman who had graduated from high school the year after Reed and I. Both of them were basketball players. The infusion of new talent helped us to quadruple our win total from the previous season to four victories, including a triumph over Barton County Community College, the team that had defeated us by 98 points my freshman year.

St. John's began a transition from a two-year to a four-year school while we were there, and Reed and I stuck around to become among the first recipients of bachelors' degrees from the college. I like to boast that I was ranked third in my class, and my roommate, Reed, was first. That sounds less impressive when I admit that there were only five students in our entire class, so I don't always bother to mention that little detail. Actually, Reed Lessing was a fine student who has become an outstanding scholar. He is a professor of Old Testament at Concordia Seminary in St. Louis, Missouri, and a prolific author. Reed is also one of the most dynamic preachers I have ever heard. We may have treated him like the runt sometimes when we were kids, but he is now a giant in my eyes, and I am proud to call him my friend.

I have always been glad to call Chris Peterson my friend. He spent two years at Creighton University in Omaha and acquitted himself very well on the basketball court. However, in the classroom he struggled a little and elected not to return to Creighton for his junior year. I twisted his arm to consider St. John's so that we could play together again. He came, he saw, he conquered. Chris became a small college All-American and shattered every St. John's scoring record in his two years on the team. The Eagles also climbed over the .500 mark for the first time in several years thanks largely to our star guard. Two years after Chris graduated he was named the head coach of the St. John's College men's basketball team—quite an achievement for a twenty-three-year-old. I was his twenty-four-year-old assistant who picked up a technical foul on the bench and got Coach Peterson tossed out of his coaching debut. With friends like that … ! Chris was the best man in my wedding, and I was the preacher for his.

My beloved alma mater closed its doors in 1986. The little college in the small town simply could not sustain sufficient enrollment to survive. The fact that I was on the staff as an admissions counselor toward the end does not say much for my recruiting abilities. Perhaps if I had spent more time concentrating on convincing high school students to come to St. John's and less time courting Johnnie alumna and admissions counselor colleague Tammy Saleska, the school would have maintained enough students to stay open! Tammy, the daughter of my psychology professor, John Saleska, did not hold against me my cash deficiency on our first date back when I was a college freshman and she was a senior at Winfield High School. However, she did play a little hard to get. I had to take up distance running in order to chase her. Our quarter-century together has seemed more like a sprint than a marathon, but I am grateful we've been in it side by side for the long run.

Professor John Saleska, simply put, is the greatest man I have ever known. Beloved teacher and devout man of God—not to mention dilettante stand-up comic—my father-in-law, in his humble, unassuming manner has had more influence on what I believe, teach, and confess than any other person. I also had him for a teacher at the seminary in Ft. Wayne, Indiana, where his career spanned more than twenty years and matched the more than two decades that he spent in Winfield teaching at St. John's.

My little sister, Kim, annoyed me when we were children by always following me around. I was pleased, however, when she followed me to St. John's to play volleyball and softball. I was absolutely delighted when she was baptized and joined the Lutheran church. So that she would not have to go through membership instruction class alone, my mother went along. Billie also decided to join the church, and so did my brother, Bill. Each of them was lovingly mentored by John Rolf, the same Lutheran pastor from our hometown who had sat at the banquet table with my parents and me our very first night in Winfield when his daughter Laura and I were welcomed as new freshman.

After I graduated from the seminary, Pastor Rolf ordained me into the ministry. I became his part-time assistant while I pursued further graduate studies in European history at the University of Colorado in Boulder. My research field was the Reformation—an interest born from my reading Roland Bainton's biography of Martin Luther during the summer after my freshman year. My brother, Bob, had purchased the paperback for me while I was living with him for a short while in Minneapolis. Now a professor of Latin American history at Boulder, Bob was an instructor for one of my graduate classes at CU. I have found the best way to succeed in school is to enroll in classes taught by your father-in-law and your brother! During the time that we were in Colorado Bob also was baptized and joined the Lutheran campus congregation in Boulder.

My most memorable duty as John Rolf's assistant was to teach the adult instruction class. Among the students was my father. Lefty was received into membership on Easter Sunday in 1988. My in-laws were in town for the holiday and in a pew among the worshippers for the Festival of the Resurrection. There we all were—John Rolf, John Saleska, Lefty, and me. The welcome banquet at St. John's College was a prelude to this moment. Better yet, it was a foretaste of the feast still to come. A vision of the eternal feast and a glimpse of glory was something that John, and John, and St. John's showed me. I had an idea to name this book, *St. John's Revelation,* but the title was already taken.

Billie already enjoys that feast in the nearer presence of Jesus so stirringly described by the original St. John's in his more famous Book of Revelation. She tastes and sees that the Lord is good. Meanwhile, I miss my mom. Rereading her letters to me during my freshman year was a poignant experience. This evidence of her tender and loving care and concern for me was profoundly moving. She has always been my inspiration and role model for what it means to be a great parent.

I have not always measured up. But, our kids mean so much to

Tammy and me. We are part of that generation of parents that drive bonkers student personnel and college administrators like me. "Helicopter parents," is what they call us, because we hover. Our overinvested interest and overactive involvement in our children's lives is made more convenient by technology and ease of communication. We don't write letters that take days to reach their destination; we send texts. We don't make calls to pay phones in college dormitories that go unanswered despite incessant ringing; we use cell phones with unlimited minutes and hit their speed dial on impulse. We don't leave our kids alone or give them much space; but we do mean well.

Neither Andrew nor any of our other four children will have a collection of letters written from me to refer to three decades from now. Most of our communications are lost somewhere in cyberspace. One reason I began to write a journal was to give them something that might fill a void the way Billie's letters have done for me. Filling the blank pages of my journal on quiet evenings at home, or in a lonely hotel room on the road, the outline for this book came to mind.

Of course, I have been processing parts of this story for more than thirty years. My New Year's resolution for 2009, the year I would turn fifty, was to pull my thoughts together before my June birthday. I began writing in January on Epiphany and finished the first full draft in April just before Easter. I gave up evenings and weekends for Lent in order to write, but it was enjoyable to see a vision begin to materialize—an epiphany come to life. It was also therapeutic. The bulk of my writing occurred during the last half of Andrew's basketball season. Thinking about what to say and how it should be said helped me to assess and analyze how I felt about what was transpiring with him. I literally did not know how Andrew's part of the story would work itself out even as I was choosing words to describe it along the way. My comments on Andrew's game against North Carolina, for instance, were being written while I watched the Tar Heels winning the national championship game against Michigan State. I'm still unsure of what comes next for him. I'd love him to come to Concordia. Wheaton still strikes me as a good choice. When the *Northwest Indiana Times* reported on changes in the Valpo roster a few weeks after the season ended, reporter Paul Oren wrote:

> As for Ferry ... the kid just wants a shot to play more than garbage time. All the stars were aligned for the Wisconsin native to contribute this season. With McPherson going down, Jones in the doghouse, and Buggs struggling with turnovers, Ferry earned double digit minutes down the stretch. He got to play against the eventual National Champions in an NBA arena. Now he's off to a smaller school (no decision has been made yet) where he can raise his value. Who knows, maybe he'll end up back at a Division I school after a year or two. What makes this case all the more heart-warming is that Ferry goes through grueling practices every day, with no promise of playing time and does so while battling diabetes.

Even as I wrote this very paragraph I paused momentarily to contact Andrew, stuck in traffic on his way home for Easter, to tell him that his AAU coach just texted me with several options to consider for college in the fall. In other words, some of this project has been and still is a moving target.

That is why the ending was abrupt—because it was not the end. Of course, that is the message of Easter—the one shared with Lefty on the day he joined the church where his son was pastor, the one shared

with Lefty, my brothers, my sister and me in that same church building at Billie's funeral, the one Andrew and his brothers and sisters and
parents will hear in a few days. The end is not the end because nothing,
not even death, separates us from God's love in Christ. In him we are
"more than conquerors," and between now and whatever comes next
"all things work together for good for those who love God and are
called according to his purpose." That was something that I learned
as a freshman at St. John's College in Winfield, Kansas.

Lefty coaches his son's basketball team. Pat kneels in the first row in front of his father.

Billie stands beside the Granada in the driveway.

The *Winfield Daily Courier* announces the signing of Patrick Ferry and Greg Levine.

St. John's Signs Basketball Duo

Two high school standout basketball players have signed letters of intent with St. John's College.

Patrick Ferry, son of Mr. and Mrs. Eugend Ferry, Denver Colo., has accepted a scholarship to attend St. John's this coming year.

Ferry attended Jefferson High School in suburban Edgewater which plays in the Jeffco league, allegedly the toughest scoring conference in Colorado, during the 1976-77 season. By averaging 12 points per game this season, he ranked among the top 20 in league scoring. He also contributed an average of 5.5 assists, 3.5 steals and four rebounds per game. For these accomplishments and his aggressive play he was named to the all-conference team and given the "top defensive player" award. Ferry is 6'1" tall, and weighs 180 lbs.

He had a 3.93 grade point average his senior year and graduated with a 3.6 cumulative grade.

Greg Levine, a standout basketball performer on the 1976-77 Detroit Lutheran West High School Team, has also enrolled at St. John's.

Leading his team to a fourth consecutive Detroit Metro conference championship, Greg lettered two years for coach Charles Boerger during 21-2 and 19-2 seasons. As an all-conference forward selection at 6'5" and 180 lbs., Greg averaged 15 points and 14 rebounds per game over the two-year period.

Patrick Ferry

Greg Levine

Chris Peterson was an all-state performer for
the Jefferson Saints.

Professor John Saleska in 1977.

An empty mailbox on
a rare day. No letters
from home.

Baden Hall,
St. John's College.

Coach Ralph Skov's St. John's team at the start of the season, including: Scott Wallace (#14) and Vince Johnson (#50) from Cleveland, Ohio. Pat Ferry is #22.

The revamped St. John's team after first semester's grade reports left only four players from the original squad. Tim Pollum (#12), Pat Ferry (back row - second from left), Paul Birner (back row - fourth from left), and Erik Skov (back row - next to his father).

Erik Skov (#20)
Pat Ferry (#22)

Pat Ferry in action
for the Eagles.

After two years at Creighton University, Chris Peterson transferred to St. John's College and became a small college All-American.

Andrew Ferry before his senior year at Milwaukee Lutheran High School.

Andrew Ferry's final high school game at Brown Deer

Gauging success by the numbers

Guard attacks diabetes, foes with great determination

By ANTHONY WITRADO
awitrado@journalsentinel.com

Halftime is always a little different for Andrew Ferry.

When the Milwaukee Lutheran boys basketball players head to the locker room and take a seat, awaiting their mid-game speech, Ferry slips off to the side.

He takes out a hand-held machine and pushes a button. A small needle shoots from the device and into Ferry's finger and quickly retracts, drawing a tiny blood sample. The machine then gives Ferry his blood-sugar level, and depending on the reading, he injects a certain amount of in-

JACK ORTON / JORTON@JOURNALSENTINEL.COM
Milwaukee Lutheran senior Andrew Ferry is among the area's top scorers.

The Milwaukee media tell the story of Andrew's battle with type 1 diabetes.

Playing on a Division I basketball team was Andrew's goal.

Andrew Ferry fires a jump shot for Valpo.

Andrew and his Valpo teammates take on the #1 ranked and eventual national champion North Carolina Tar Heels.

Homer Drew's team celebrates the coach's six hundredth career victory. Andrew Ferry stands in the middle of the three players to Coach Drew's right side.

CITATIONS

I gratefully acknowledge the following sources for articles, blogs, excerpts, photographs, and other materials that have helped me to tell the story:

Journal Sentinel, Milwaukee, WI

Ken Gaschk Photographs

Northwest Indiana Times, Munster, IN (Valparaiso, IN)

Post-Tribune of Northwest Indiana, Merrillville, IN

St. John's Alumni Association, Winfield, KS

Visual Image Photography, Wauwatosa, WI

Valparaiso University Athletic Department, Valparaiso, IN

Winfield Daily Courier, Winfield, KS

ABOUT THE AUTHOR

Patrick Ferry has been president of Concordia University Wisconsin since 1997. He joined the history faculty at Concordia in 1991. Most of his previous publications include essays and articles in journals and books relating to European history, higher education, and Christian faith and life. Pat and his wife, Tammy, are parents to five children. They make their home in Wauwatosa, Wisconsin—a suburb of Milwaukee.